BASIC GUITAR

THE TAB-ONLY GUITAR METHOD! By ALEX DAVIS

Amsco Publications

a part of *The* **Music Sales** *Group*

New York/Los Angeles/Nashville/London/Berlin/Copenhagen/Madrid/Paris/Sydney/Tokyo

Acknowledgements:

I would like to thank my family, particularly my wonderful parents, for their endless support, encouragement, and tolerance of my musical endeavors over the years. Many thanks also to Heather Ramage and David Bradley at Music Sales for their inspired editing and reckless confidence in my writing abilities; to my teachers, mentors, and colleagues past and present; and to my friends throughout the world.

Cover design by Stacy Boge
Project Editors: Heather Ramage and David Bradley
Interior design and layout by Len Vogler
CD produced by Felipe Orozco
Engineered by Tae Gyun Kim

Order No. AM 983290
ISBN-10: 0.8256.3466.0
ISBN-13: 978.0.8256.3466.6

Exclusive Distributors:
Music Sales Corporation
257 Park Avenue South, New York, NY 10010 USA
Music Sales Limited
14-15 Berners Street, London W1T 3LJ England
Music Sales Pty. Limited
120 Rothschild Street, Rosebery, Sydney, NSW 2018, Australia

Printed in the United States of America by
Vicks Lithograph and Printing Corporation

Table of Contents

4 CD Track Listing

Why are you reading *Basic Guitar: The TAB-Only Guitar Method?*

Simple answer:

You DON'T want to wade through a sea of complicated and confusing music theory, having to learn all about those dots, squiggles, and Italian words before you can call yourself a guitarist.

But...

You DO want to learn to play one of the most fun, versatile, simple, and incredibly cool musical instruments ever invented.

You DO want to be able to read and write *TAB*—simple music notation designed by guitarists for guitarists, available in shops worldwide and all over the Internet.

You DO want to equip yourself with the skills and techniques to master the tunes you love, and be able to jam with other musicians easily and confidently.

You DO want to know your guitar backwards, forwards, inside-out and upside-down, how to care for it and what to buy to go with it.

This book will help you with all of these things and more. Learning to play a musical instrument is one of the most rewarding and enjoyable experiences in the world, and there are very few instruments that are as flexible in terms of what you can play, how you can play it, and who you can play it with as the guitar.

And although it will take practice and a little patience, it's not going to be as hard as you might think...

Guitar Anatomy

All guitars are formed of two main components: the body and the neck. *Acoustic* guitars have a hollow body that amplifies the sound of the strings' vibrations. *Electric* guitars have solid or semi-hollow bodies, and use magnetic pickups to turn the sound of the strings into small electric currents, which are fed down a cable and into an amplifier to make more noise.

Electro-acoustic guitars can amplify the sound of the strings in either way, with *piezo* (contact) pickups built into or under the bridge rather than magnetic pickups under the strings.

Electric Guitar

Parts of the Guitar (Electric and Acoustic)

1. Headstock. The end of the neck that holds the tuning pegs.
2. Tuning pegs. These are turned to tighten or slacken the strings, changing the tuning.
3. Nut. Small piece of plastic, bone, or metal at the bottom of the headstock that keeps the strings in the correct position over the fretboard.
4. Strings. The metal wires you play to make music!
5. Fretboard (or fingerboard). Thin piece of wood attached to the front of the neck that holds the frets.
6. Frets. Thin strips of metal built into the fretboard. Holding a string against a fret changes its vibrating length, altering its pitch.
7. Fret markers. These dots help you find the correct position on the neck more easily.
8. Strap pin. This is where you attach one end of your guitar strap—sometimes located on the heel of the neck on some electrics and acoustics. Not all steel-string acoustics have a strap pin here.
9. Pickups. Magnetic devices that turn the vibrations of the strings into an electric current, which is then fed down a cable into an amplifier.
10. Pickguard. This prevents you from damaging the front of your guitar (sometimes known as the "top") with your pick when strumming. Usually made from plastic.
11. Bridge. This anchors the ball-ends of the strings to the body of the guitar. Electro-acoustic guitars have a pickup built into or under the bridge.
12. Endpin. This is where you attach the other end of the guitar strap. On many electro-acoustic guitars, the endpin also houses the output jack.
13. Pickup selector. A switch allowing you to choose which pickup(s) you want to use, creating different tones.
14. Volume/Tone controls. Allow you to alter the volume and tone of the sound from the pickups. Electro-acoustic guitars usually have these on the top side of the body, sometimes mounted in a little panel.
15. Output jack. The socket where you attach a cable to go to an amplifier. Also found on electro-acoustic guitars.

Here we have two of the world's most common styles of guitars (an electric guitar on the left, and an acoustic guitar on the right), which between them have all the parts you're ever likely to find on a guitar.

You should also be aware of your guitar's *action,* or the height of the strings from the fretboard. This is adjusted by altering the angle of the neck and the height of the bridge—most good guitar shops will be able to "set up" the action of your guitar for you.

Acoustic Guitar

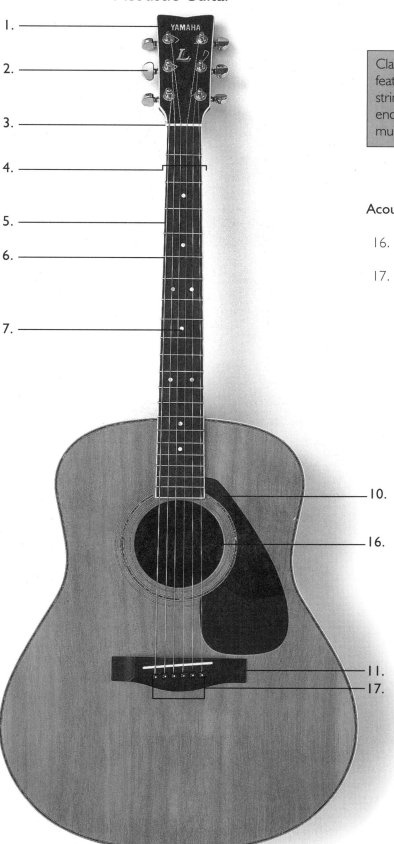

1.
2.
3.
4.
5.
6.
7.
10.
16.
11.
17.

Classical/Spanish/flamenco guitars share almost all of the features of steel-string acoustic guitars, but have nylon strings instead of metal, usually don't have any strap- or endpins at all, are far lighter in construction, and feature a much wider fretboard.

Acoustic Guitar Only

16. Soundhole. Opening on the face of the guitar through which sound is projected.
17. Bridge pins. These hold the ball-ends of the strings in place below the bridge.

Holding Your Guitar

The golden rule here is that you should be comfortable, whether you decide to stand or sit with your guitar. In either case, you should always keep the neck of the guitar pointing slightly upward, and NEVER downward. Avoid tensing your arms and back—a relaxed guitarist is a happy guitarist. This book has been written with right-handed guitarists in mind— apologies to all you left-handed readers, who should simply reverse any right- or left-hand instructions.

Sitting

Sit the guitar on your right leg, keeping the body nestled comfortably somewhere in the crook of your right arm. This way, you'll support the instrument while keeping both hands free to play.

Standing

Try to keep the strap length sensible so the guitar is positioned at the level of your waist rather than slung somewhere below your crotch, no matter how much you may want to look like a rock star (this is something you can try later on). You want the guitar to support and balance itself on the strap without your having to hold onto it at all.

This is something you'll probably need to do each and every time you pick up your guitar. If each string isn't at the correct pitch before you start playing, then everything is going to sound a bit off. The six strings should be tuned (from low to high) E–A–D–G–B–E, and here are four ways of doing it:

Tuning to the CD

Track  of the CD that comes with this book features all six strings being played one after another from low to high. Play through the strings, tuning each one until the notes from your guitar match the notes on the CD. Turn the peg towards the back of the guitar to tighten the string and raise the pitch, and turn the peg towards the front of the guitar to loosen the string and lower the pitch.

Tuning to a piano or keyboard

A well-tuned acoustic piano, or an electric piano or keyboard, provides an ideal tool for tuning a guitar. This diagram shows you which keys correspond to which strings.

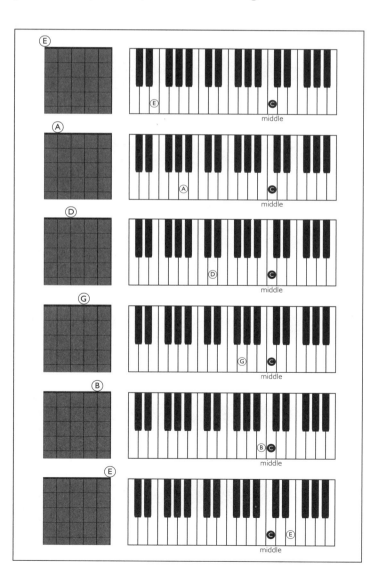

Tuning to an electronic tuner

Probably the easiest way to tune your guitar, an electronic tuner either plugs into your electric guitar or picks up the notes from your acoustic guitar through a microphone, telling you exactly what note you're playing and whether or not you need to tune up or down. Many tuners even know which string you're trying to tune as well!

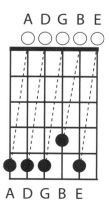

Relative tuning

You can tune the guitar to itself by matching fretted notes to open strings. Following the diagram below, here's how you would tune the guitar to the low E string:

1. Hold the low E string (sixth string) down at the fifth fret and play it along with the open A string (fifth string). Turn the tuning peg for the A string until the two notes match—the A string is now in tune.
2. Hold the A string (fifth string) down at the fifth fret and tune the open D string (fourth string) to it.
3. Hold the D string (fourth string) down at the fifth fret and tune the open G string (third string) to it.
4. Hold the G string (third string) down at the *fourth* fret and tune the open B string (second string) to it.
5. Hold the B string (second string) down at the fifth fret and tune the open E string (first string) to it.

A D G B E

A D G B E

Left Hand

Keep your thumb comfortably behind the neck, roughly parallel to your first and second fingers—try not to rest your palm against the neck:

Your fingers should be relaxed and slightly bent, with well-trimmed nails:

The fingers of the left hand are numbered 1 through 4:

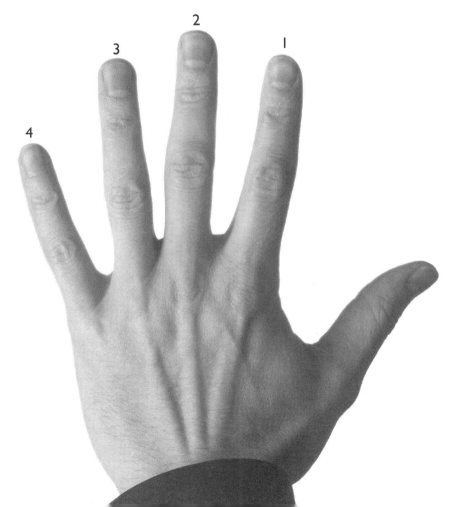

Right Hand

Most guitarists strum the guitar with a small piece of plastic called a *pick* (or *plectrum*), which should be held firmly between the thumb and the side of the index finger—it will feel a bit weird at first! It's better to use a lighter, more flexible pick to start.

You strum both down and up when playing the guitar. Try strumming up and down a few times to get used to the movement. Relax your whole arm and let your hand brush across the strings as it falls—the movement should be from the elbow.

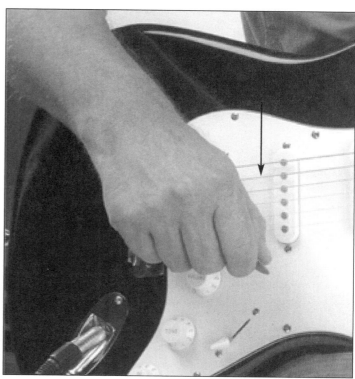

Strum the guitar with a pick, your thumb, or your fingernails (pinch your thumb and index finger together to make an "instant pick"). Keep your wrist hovering over the strings just in front of the bridge so that your fingers will naturally strum the guitar just in front of the neck (or over the soundhole of an acoustic guitar).

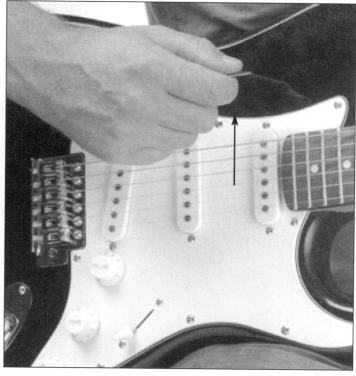

Amplifiers

If you have an electric guitar, you'll also need an amplifier and a guitar cable to get a sound out of your instrument. Here's a step-by-step guide to setting up:

1. Attach your guitar strap. Make sure that the strap is adjusted to a comfortable length. A low-slung guitar looks really cool but is actually much more difficult to play—as long as your right and left hands feel comfortable on the guitar your position is probably right.

2. Plug one end of your guitar cable into the guitar. On a Les Paul-type guitar (as shown here) the output jack is on the underside of the body of the guitar. On a Fender Stratocaster type you will find the output jack on the front of the guitar under the tone controls.

3. Take the other end of the cable and plug it into the jack marked "input" on your amplifier.

4. Adjust the volume controls on the amplifier and on your guitar until you can hear a sound from the amplifier.

If you can't hear any sound, check that the amp is plugged in and switched on, and that the volume control on your guitar is turned up.

Now you're ready to play!

If you're lucky enough to have an effects unit such as a distortion or wah-wah pedal you can have even more fun!

Effects pedals take the sound from your guitar and change it before it gets passed on to the amplifier. They can be powered by batteries or by a separate power supply.

Take the other end of the cable that is plugged into your guitar and insert it into the input jack on the pedal (sometimes marked "instrument").

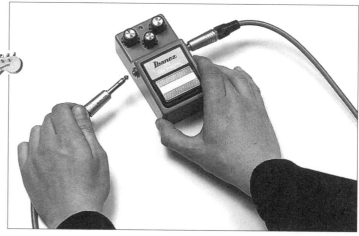

Then take another cable and connect the output jack on the pedal to the input jack on the amp.

The pedal is activated by simply stomping on the foot-operated switch. When the pedal is not switched on you should still be able hear the sound of your guitar as before—when you step on the switch the sound should change as the effect kicks in!

Once you're happy with your guitar set-up, turn up the volume and make some noise!

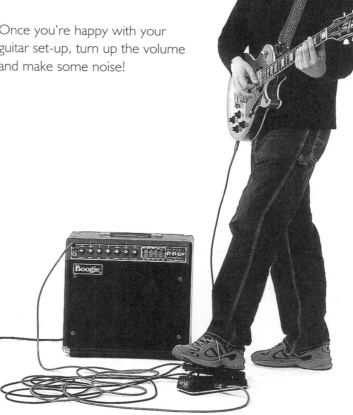

A wah-wah pedal produces a classic effect that you'll recognize instantly. You can plug it in in the same way as other effects pedals, and then vary the tone of your guitar sound by rocking back and forth on the pedal.

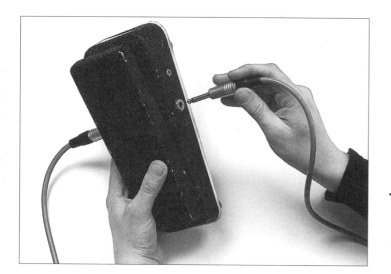

Chord boxes and guitar tablature (or "TAB," as it's commonly called) are two fantastically simple ways of writing and reading music for guitar. Both are basically graphical representations of your guitar neck—instead of showing notes in a traditional sense, they show frets and strings, and both tell you EXACTLY where your fingers should go. Chord boxes are there to show you how to play individual chords, while TAB can be used to show any kind of guitar music. TAB is especially effective at showing lead guitar solos and melodies. More on this later…

This is an A major chord, shown on the guitar neck and as a chord box.

And here's the same A major chord, this time written in TAB. The six lines (called a *staff*) represent the six strings of the guitar from the player's viewpoint (strings 6 through 1, from bottom to top, thick string to thin string, or E–A–D–G–B–E), and the numbers on the lines tell you which fret to play, with a zero ("0") written for an open string. If there are no numbers on a string then you don't play that string. Even simpler!

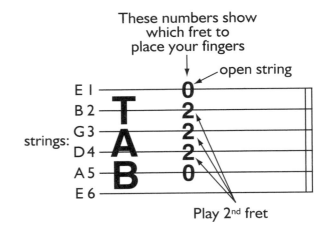

These numbers show which fret to place your fingers

open string

strings:

Play 2nd fret

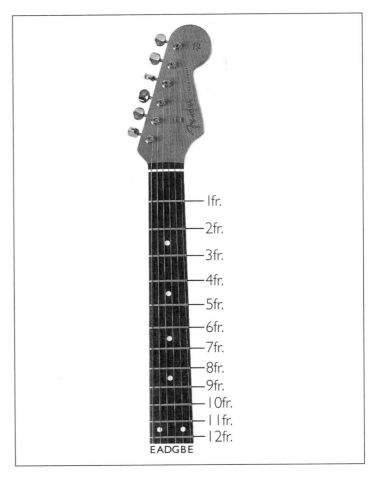

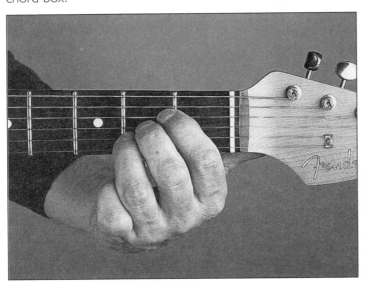

A

Play this string open
(no fingers on the frets)

Do not play this string

Nut

These circles show you where to put your fingers

The number inside tells you which finger to use

① ② ③

frets

strings: 6 5 4 3 2 1
        E A D G B E

You can also write individual notes as guitar TAB. Here is the A major chord again with each individual note picked from bottom to top, one after another. A chord performed like this (each note played separately) is known as an *arpeggio*.

Now that you've seen the A major chord written down in two different ways, it's time to actually try playing it:

Look carefully at how the fingers are positioned in this picture, lined up one after the other and pointing directly down at the fingerboard—you should aim to press the strings down with the very tips of your fingers, keeping your hand slightly arched.

The strings should be held down just behind the fret. NEVER place your fingers directly on the metal strips. Try playing each individual string by itself before you put them all together. That way, each of your fingers will get used to doing what they should be.

Remember that you're not playing the sixth string (thick E string) in this chord, so start your downstroke from the fifth string (A string) all the way down the rest of the strings.

Don't worry if playing this chord feels weird—remember that you're teaching your fingers to bend and position themselves in ways that they're simply not used to. Sore fingertips are also natural when learning the guitar—they're not accustomed to being rubbed and pressed against metal wires on a regular basis! The more you practice, the more your hands and fingers will toughen and adapt to what you're asking of them.

If your chord seems buzzy or muffled in any way, then it's probably due to one of the following reasons:

1. Your fingers might not be holding the strings down firmly enough.

2. Your fingers may be too close to the frets themselves (perhaps even accidentally ON the frets).

3. At least one of your fingers may be touching or brushing against the string next to the one it's supposed to be playing, preventing it from vibrating properly. In this case it's likely to be your third finger brushing the top E string (first string) or your first finger brushing the A string (fifth string).

4. You're not keeping the fingernails on your fretting hand trimmed properly, and it's these that are either catching adjacent strings or preventing your fingers from holding down the strings down properly. Either way, trim your fingernails!

Introduction to Rhythm

All music is made up of notes and rhythm, and while plain TAB is a good way of writing notes, it unfortunately doesn't show you what rhythm to play the notes in.

To solve this problem we will include a one-line rhythm staff above the TAB containing *rhythm slashes* that show you how long to play each note.

The different kinds of rhythm slashes indicate different note durations, all of which are conveniently linked to one another in terms of length.

Each rhythm slash also has a corresponding *rest* symbol, indicating a point in time where you shouldn't play anything! Here we have a rhythm tree with the corresponding rest symbols, showing you how all the rhythm slashes and rests are written and related.

The whole notes at the top of the tree are held for the longest duration and the notes at the bottom are held for the shortest. There are notes even quicker than sixteenth notes, but you will not need them for this book.

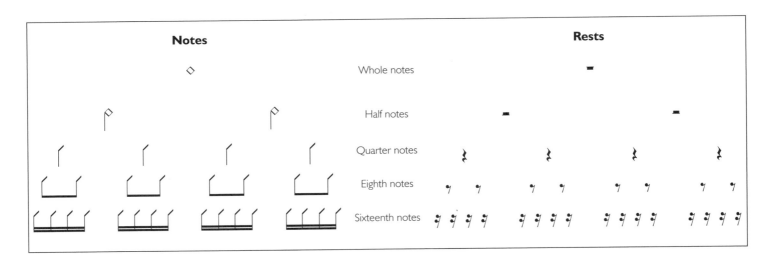

So adding the rhythm staff to our TAB staff gives us something like this:

Tracks 2 & 3

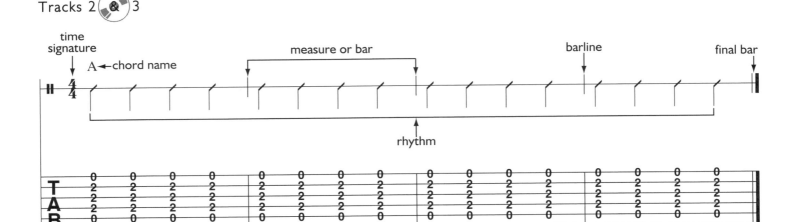

The vertical lines (*barlines*) drawn on the staves divide the music into *measures* (or *bars*). This makes the music easier to read, as you will discover.

The $\frac{4}{4}$ written at the start of the rhythm staff is called the *time signature*—the bottom number indicates the type of beat duration used (quarter notes in this case) and the top number shows how many of these beats there are in each measure (four in this case).

The four beats in each measure are marked to illustrate the rhythms more clearly.

Listen to the above tune on **Track 2**, and then try playing along with **Track 3**.

D Major Chord and a Few Downstrokes

Time for another chord: D major. This chord only uses four notes, so only strum the top four strings on your guitar, leaving out strings 5 and 6 (A and the thick E string).

This may look a little trickier to play than the A major chord you've already learned, but don't let the more complicated-looking finger positioning fool you—it's actually much easier to play. Remember to use the tips of your fingers as before!

The different ways you position your fingers to play different chords are known as *chord shapes*—this particular chord shape should prove much less troublesome to perform without accidental buzzing and muting of strings than the A major chord. Just be careful not to brush the top E string (first string) or the G string (third string) with your third finger while it's holding down the B string (second string), and make sure your first finger doesn't brush the open D string (fourth string).

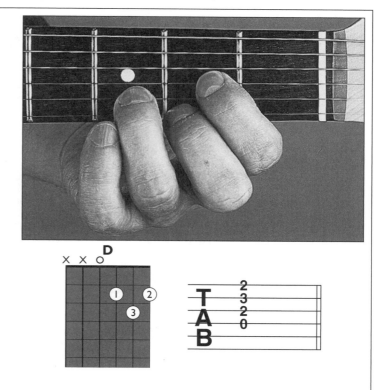

Another thing that TAB music can show you is how to strum particular chords. A ⊓ symbol above a chord tells you to play that chord with a downstroke—from the top of the guitar to the bottom.

Notice how playing all the chords with downstrokes gives them a very distinctive feel, especially when playing a fast collection of eighth notes like these.

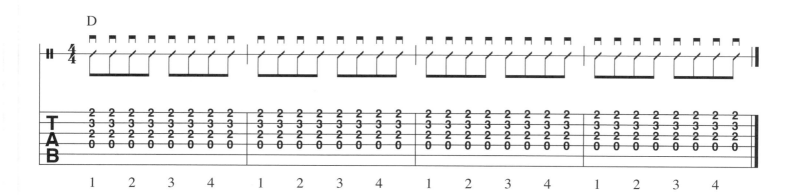

E Major Chord and a Few Upstrokes

A nice, BIG, easy chord for you now: E major, which uses ALL the strings on your guitar so you don't have to worry too much about aiming your pick!

Watch out for potential string buzzes caused by your third finger rubbing against the G string (third string), or your first finger rubbing against the B string (second string). Otherwise, there is very little that can go wrong when playing this one.

Since we're now playing all the strings together, it's time to start strumming down and up. A ∨ symbol above a chord tells you to play that chord with an upstroke—from the bottom of the guitar (thinner strings) to the top (thicker strings).

Notice how all the downstrokes fall directly *on* each beat while the upstrokes are played between (or *off*) each beat. This is how most guitar tunes are strummed, regardless of style or time signature, so playing in this way is definitely a good habit to get into. Have a listen to this short section being played on **Track 4** and try it yourself along with **Track 5,** getting into your new strumming pattern and enjoying the fact that you can hit all the strings together at last!

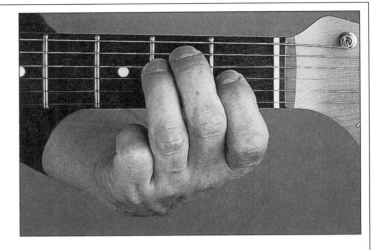

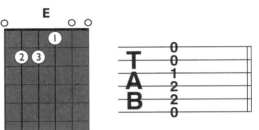

Tracks 4 & 5

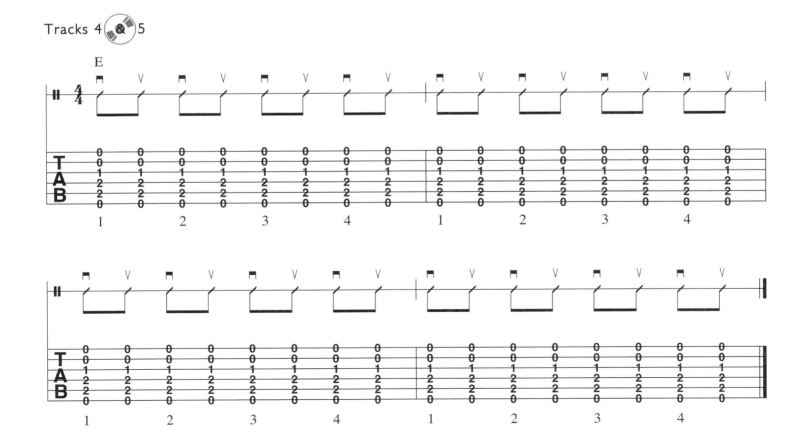

Chord Review

We're almost ready to take all your newly acquired skills and put them together in a few tunes, but first let's have another quick play through our A, D, and E major chords.

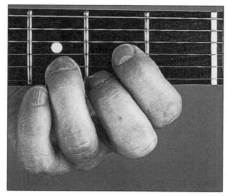

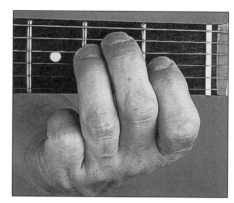

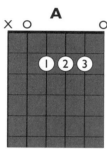

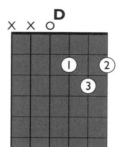

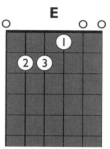

It's worth taking some time to practice playing these three chords one after another in different orders for a little while before you try out the TAB written below. Your fingers have adapted themselves to the different chord shapes they've played so far, but now need to be able to change between these shapes quickly and accurately.

You can use this tune to practice your chord changes. Take it nice and slow at first and then work the speed up a little. Have a listen to it being played on **Track 6** and then have a go yourself with **Track 7** when you're ready.

Tracks 6 & 7

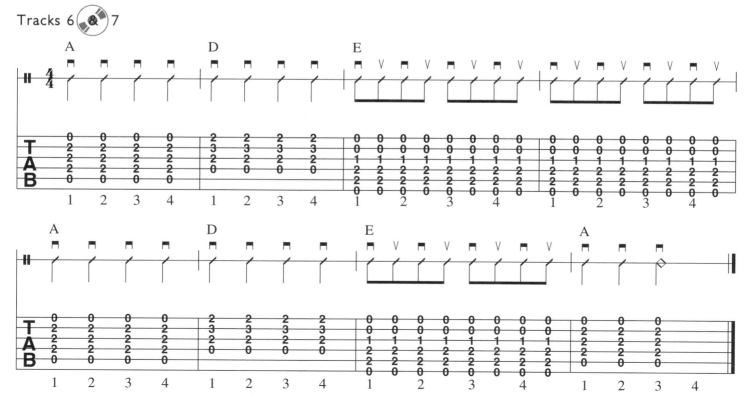

Three Tunes with A, D, and E

Repeat Signs

Now let's throw a few quarter-note rests into your music. This tune uses just the E and A major chords, and introduces you to *repeat signs*, which are barlines that bracket a section of music to be repeated.

The *backward* repeat barline (:|) tells you to go back to the *forward* repeat barline (|:), or to the beginning, and play the section again. Have a listen to this tune being played on **Track 8** and then try it yourself with **Track 9**.

Tracks 8  9

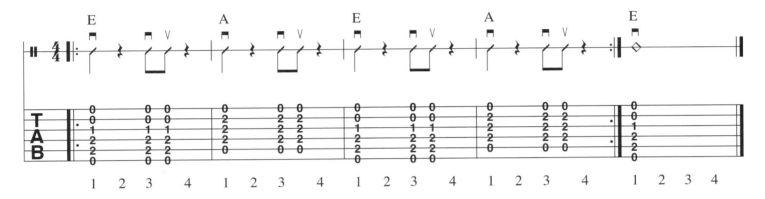

Here's a slightly faster rock tune that will help you to practice different strumming patterns and quicker chord changes.

Have a listen to this tune being played on **Track 10** and give it a try yourself with **Track 11**.

Tracks 10 & 11

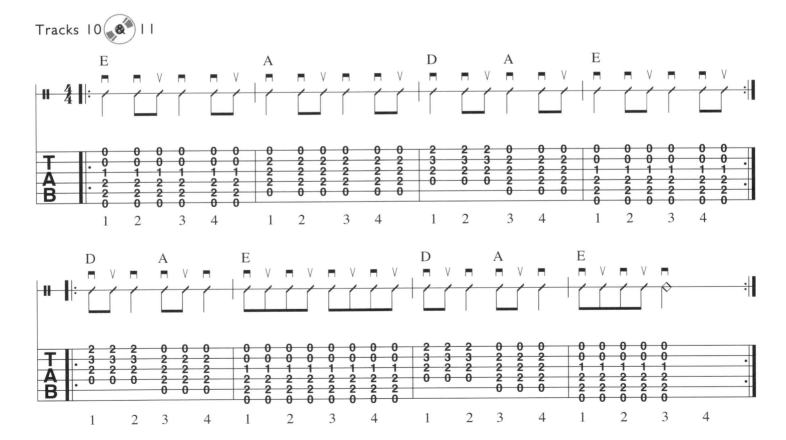

G Major

Another "big" but easy chord is G major, and this is where you're going to have to start stretching those fingers out a bit more!

There are two possible fingerings for this chord. You could use fingers 2, 3, and 4 rather than 1, 2, and 3 as shown here. This alternative fingering will make the change from C to G smoother. Experiment and see what works best for you.

Remember to curl your fingers over the fingerboard so that your fingertips are coming straight down onto the strings. If your fingertips lean over one way or the other, you might accidentally mute an adjacent string that needs to ring out.

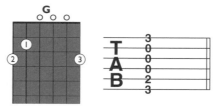

C Major

Now for the C major chord—not quite as much stretching needed here thankfully.

We're only playing the top five strings with this chord (as with A major) and your finger placement needs to be especially careful since there needs to be an open G string (fourth string) vibrating between your first and second fingers, not to mention the open thin E string at the top of the chord.

This leaves far more opportunity for accidental string buzzes to occur, so make sure you're keeping your hand arched and are using the tips of your fingers to hold the strings down.

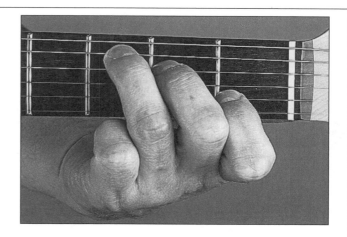

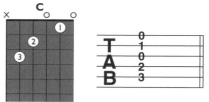

Two New Chords and a New Time Signature

A New Time Signature: $\frac{3}{4}$

We'll try playing these two new chords in a new time signature—the $\frac{3}{4}$ at the start of the staff means there are three quarter notes to every bar, giving you a "1–2–3, 1–2–3" rhythm (sometimes called *waltz time*).

Don't forget the repeats! Have a listen to this tune being played on **Track 12** and give it a try yourself along with **Track 13**.

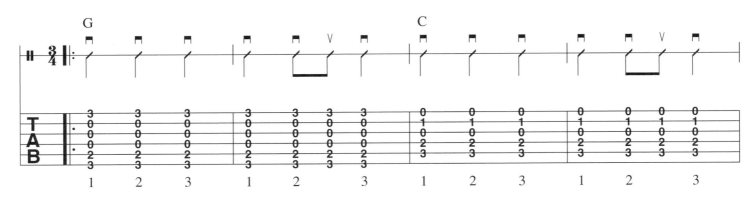

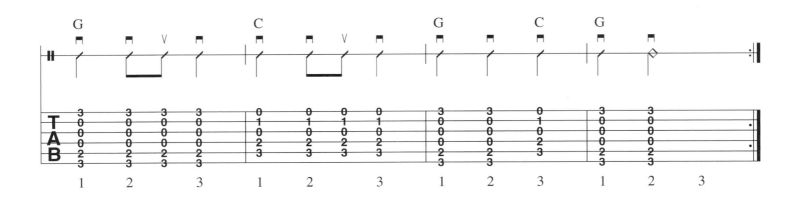

What you have learned so far!

- Parts of the guitar (and what they all do)
- How to tune your guitar
- How to hold your guitar
- Right- and left-hand positions
- How to set up your amp and effects
- How to read TAB and chord boxes
- How to read rhythm
- Five chords: A, D, E, G, and C
- Tunes in $\frac{4}{4}$ and $\frac{3}{4}$ time
- Down- and upstrokes

Two New Chords and a New Time Signature

Now we'll mix in our E major and A major chords as well, and speed things up just a little. This tune has a nice "floaty" feel to it so try to keep your strumming fairly light. The ⌢ symbol over the final chord indicates a pause (called a *fermata*).

You should hold this note for a little longer than written (or however long you WANT to hold it for). Listen to this tune being played on **Track 14** and try it yourself with **Track 15**.

Tracks 14  15

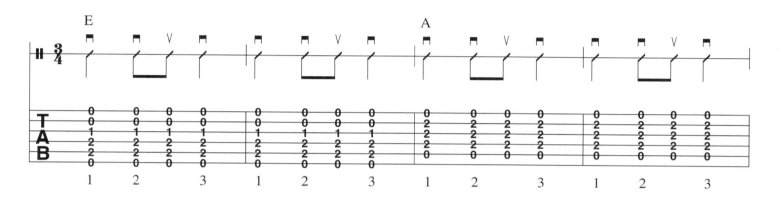

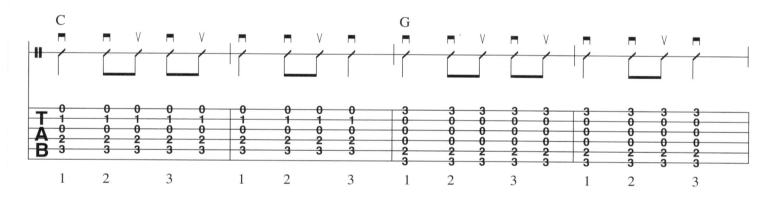

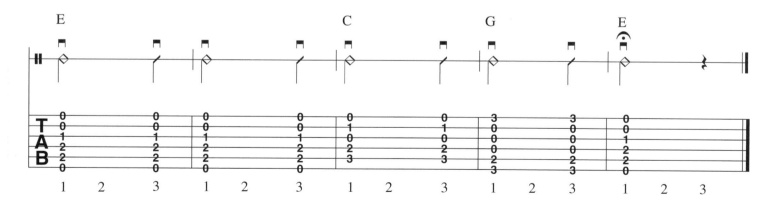

The five chords you've learned so far are all *major* chords, so it's time to add a couple of *minor* chords to your collection.

The difference between the two is that minor chords have a "darker" quality about them.

E Minor

We'll start with the easiest one of all: E minor.

Undoubtedly the simplest chord you've looked at so far—all the strings are strummed, only two fingers are required, and it's very easy to play without any buzzing problems (assuming you're keeping your fingers and hand positioned correctly, of course). As shown in the chord boxes, you can use either your second and third fingers or your first and second fingers to play this one, depending on what you're more comfortable with (try it out both ways). This is very similar to the E major chord, but without the first finger holding down the G string (third string) at the first fret (this is what makes it *minor*).

Play E major and then E minor one after the other and hear the difference.

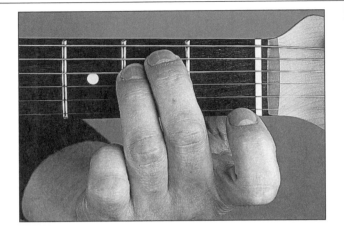

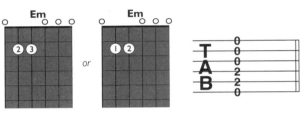

We'll first use our E minor chord in this gentle section of music which should get you used to changing between the E minor and G major chord shapes—quite common in guitar tunes.

Have a listen to this tune being played on **Track 16** and give it a try yourself with **Track 17**.

Tracks 16  17

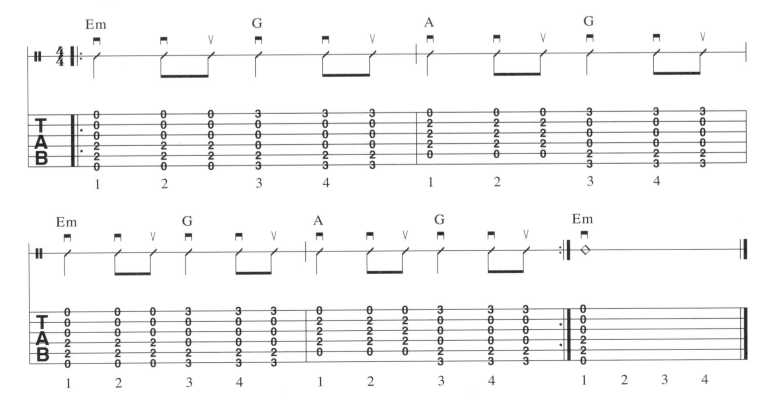

And now for a faster section with slightly trickier chord changes.

Have a listen to this tune being played on **Track 18** and try it yourself along with **Track 19.**

Tracks 18 & 19

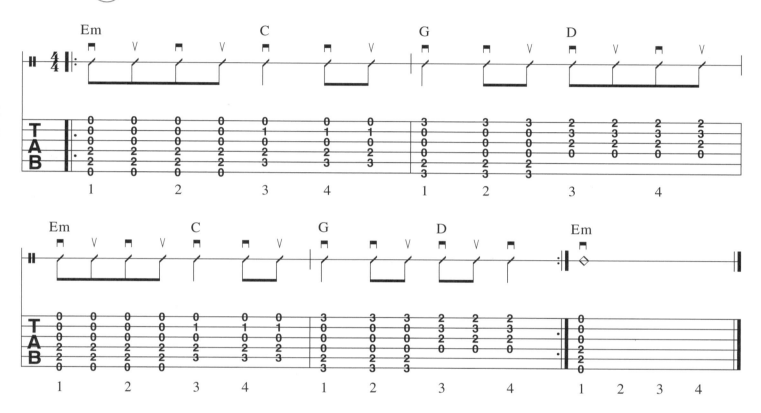

A Minor

Now for another chord that's also similar to E major, but in a completely different way.

The three-finger chord shape for A minor is identical to that of E major—you simply move the entire shape over one set of strings (toward the floor) and leave out the thick E string (sixth string) completely.

Although it only differs from the A major chord by one fret, it does require a completely different fingering, and be careful of string buzzes happening on the B string and thin open E string (second and first strings).

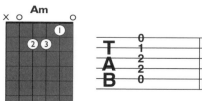

Ties and Syncopation

We'll start joining or *tying* notes together at this point to change the feel of the rhythms you're playing.

A *tie* (‿ or ⌢) between notes or chords tells you to hold the note or chord for the entire length of all the notes connected by the tie.

The tie is only written in the rhythm staff; the TAB staff just displays the first of the tied notes or chords that you should play and hold for the length of the tied rhythm slashes.

Notice the way that the first tied note in each measure anticipates and emphasizes the third beat—this is called *syncopation*.

Try to keep the up-down, eighth-note strumming motion in your right hand constant throughout this tune even when you're not actually hitting any strings, such as on the third beat of each measure, where you'd "play" a silent downstroke—this is known as an *air-stroke*.

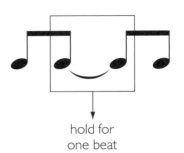

hold for
one beat

Here's a short exercise for you to try the easy chord change between E major and A minor, with a few ties thrown in.

Have a listen to this tune being played on **Track 20** and try it yourself with **Track 21**.

Tracks 20  21

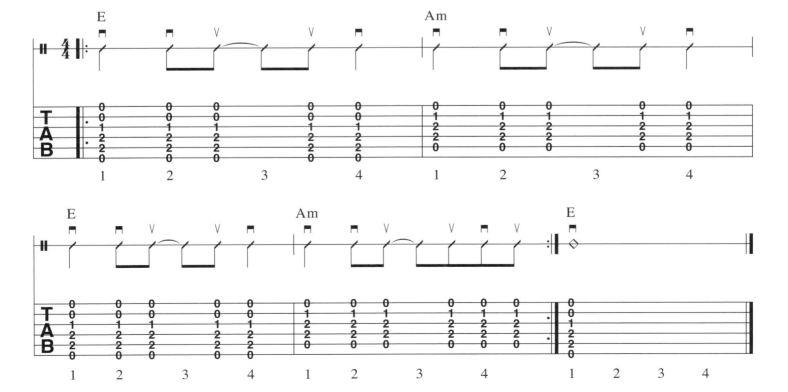

Here's an all-in-one tune for you to tackle, featuring rests, ties, syncopation, and some lovely chord changes to sink your teeth into. Notice that it's possible to tie notes and chords across barlines!

All the rests in this tune can be accomplished by muting the strings with the palm of your right hand on the downstroke. Listen to this tune being played on **Track 22** and give it a try yourself along with **Track 23**.

Tracks 22 & 23

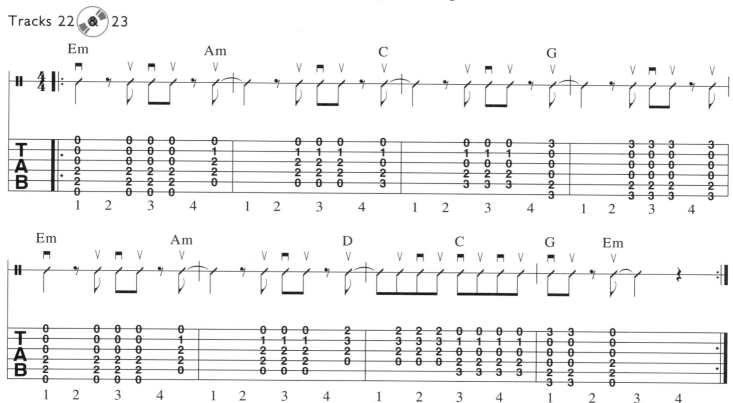

Now for a few sixteenth notes—take this tune very slowly and play it very gently.

There's a good chance that your eighth-note strumming motion will naturally turn into a sixteenth-note strumming motion with this tune—this is perfectly fine!

Tracks 24 & 25

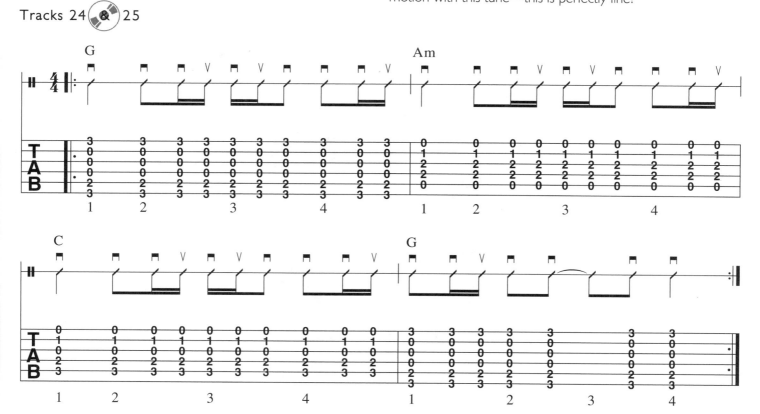

D Minor

By now your fingers should be accustomed to forming chord shapes, so here's a D minor chord for you to try.

The wonderful thing about D major and D minor is that you only have to hold down the really thin strings, making them both very "light" chords to play. This chord differs from D major by just one fret and similarly uses only the top four strings on your guitar, so be careful not to strum the A and low E (fifth and sixth strings).

Any buzzing problems you may have with this one are probably caused by your third finger rubbing against either the first string or third string, so be careful.

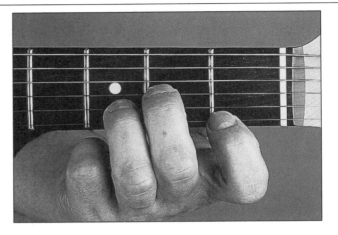

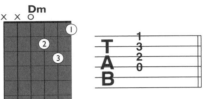

Another New Time Signature: $\frac{6}{8}$

We'll bring in a new time signature at this point, $\frac{6}{8}$, which gives you six eighth notes to every measure. This actually gives you exactly the same amount of beats per bar as a $\frac{3}{4}$ time signature (think about it!) but in a completely different feel.

This country-style tune gives you a nice easy chord change from A minor to D minor, which only requires a small change in finger positioning. Listen to this tune on **Track 26** and give it a try yourself with **Track 27**.

Tracks 26  27

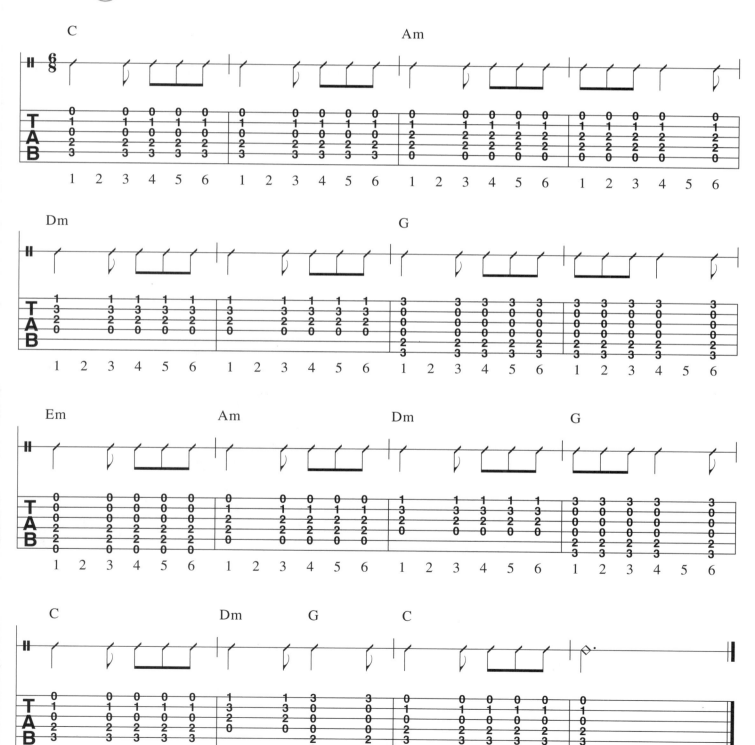

Now for something completely different: *7th* chords! These are technically known as *dominant 7th* chords, which distinguish them from *minor 7th* and *major 7th* chords (we'll come to those later).

E7

Here's our first dominant chord, E7.

What we have here is essentially an E major chord with the third finger removed, allowing the open D string to provide the seventh note of the scale, which gives that nice blues/jazz sound to the whole thing.

Practice strumming E7 in the following pattern:

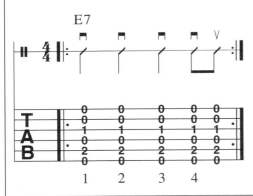

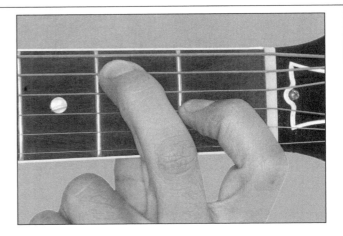

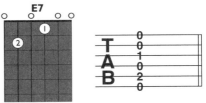

A7

Now for an A7 chord.

Again, this is the same as an A major chord but with the G string left open to provide that jazzy-sounding seventh note.

Practice strumming A7 in the following pattern:

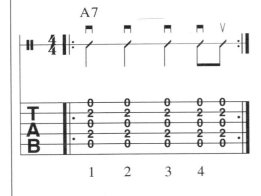

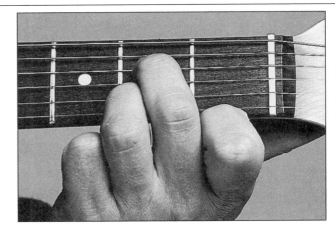

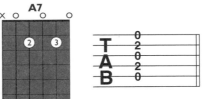

B7

Now for the B7 chord (and this is where things get a bit more complicated):

Although this chord is totally different from everything we've seen so far, it's still pretty simple to play. Remember not to strum the thick E string (sixth string) and watch out for your third and fourth fingers accidentally rubbing against the open B string (second string).

Practice strumming B7 in the following pattern:

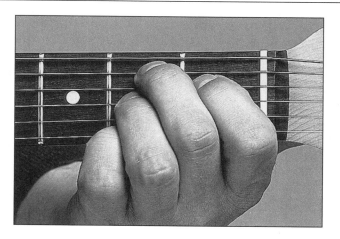

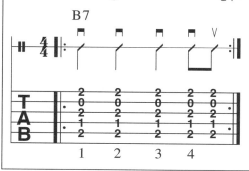

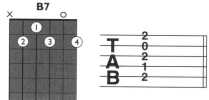

Swing Feel

Before we tackle the next chord sequence, we need to learn about *swing feel*. This is where we take "even" or "straight" eighth notes and play them with a sort of bounce—almost a $\frac{6}{8}$ feel in fact—where the first eighth note is a little longer and the second eighth is a little shorter.

Jazz and blues music is almost always performed with a swing to it, and since most modern popular music has its roots in jazz or blues, it's definitely worth getting used to playing your guitar in this style. Try playing this rhythm on your guitar using any chord or string.

This line of eighth notes:

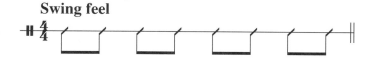

Should sound like THIS when you swing them:

First and Second Endings

We're also going to add *1st-* and *2nd-time* endings to your music. These are devices to make your repeats more interesting. The repeat section should end the first time around with the bar marked ⌐1. ⌐.

The second time around you should skip this bar and play the bar marked ⌐2. ⌐, which ends the tune in this case.

Dominant 7ᵗʰ Chords

Now you're ready to try this basic *twelve-bar blues* (probably the most common *chord progression* in guitar music). Make sure you keep it relaxed.

Check out this tune on **Track 28** and try it yourself with **Track 29**.

Tracks 28  29

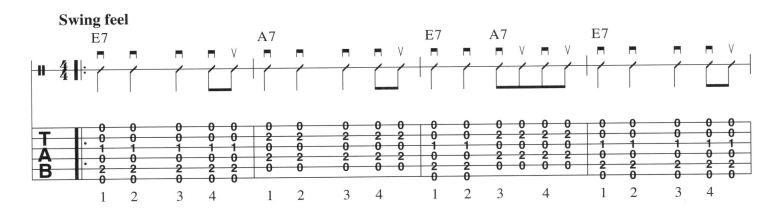

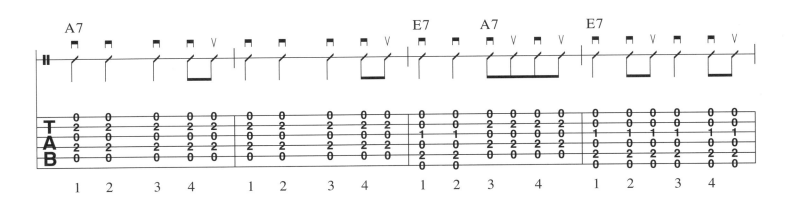

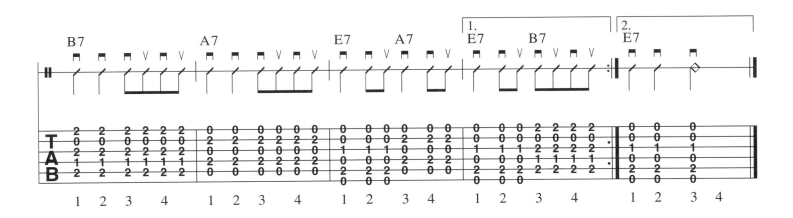

D7

Another 7th chord for your collection is D7.

Again, we are only using the top four strings of the guitar to play D7, as with all our D chords so far, and it's just as light on the fingers. The chord shape for this one is almost a mirror image of the D major chord shape, with the B string held down at the first fret rather than the third.

Practice strumming D7 in the following pattern:

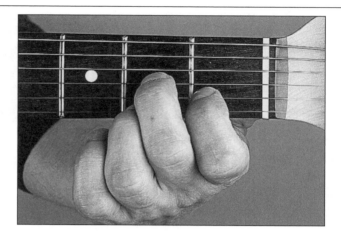

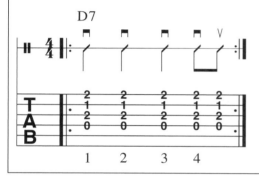

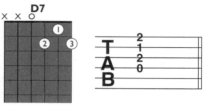

Augmentation Dots

Before we include our D7 chord in a tune, let's take a look at a couple of interesting things you can do with *dots* in your music.

First, we have dotted rhythms. An *augmentation dot* written directly to the right of a rhythm slash extends the length of that note by half—a dotted quarter note would sound for the same length as a quarter note tied to an eighth note (see example below).

Using dotted rhythms cuts down on the need for quite so many tied notes, making your music less cluttered and easier to read.

Staccato Dots

Dots positioned directly above or below the rhythm slash (and above the TAB) tell you to play *staccato*, which means you should make the written notes or chords sound as short as possible (see example below).

This is usually done by muting the string(s) with the fingers of your left hand or the palm of your right hand immediately after plucking or strumming.

Dominant 7th Chords

Here are ALL your 7th chords mixed in with staccato notes, dotted rhythms, and a healthy dose of syncopation, wrapped up in one tune!

This one is nice and heavy so don't be afraid to attack the strings. Listen to **Track 30** and then try it yourself along with **Track 31**.

Tracks 30  31

Minor 7th chords sound even "bluesier" than dominant 7th chords—perhaps because, like all minor chords, they sound "sadder."

Strum through these different chords at your own pace, changing between them at random.

Em7

We'll start with Em7, a chord which can be played in a variety of ways. All the strings are strummed and only one finger is required on the fretboard (and it doesn't even matter which finger you use).

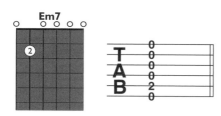

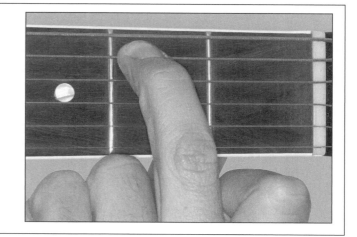

Am7

Now for Am7. This chord is very similar to A minor—you're just removing your third finger and allowing the G string to be played open, and don't forget to leave out the E string in your strum.

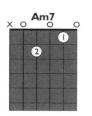
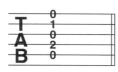

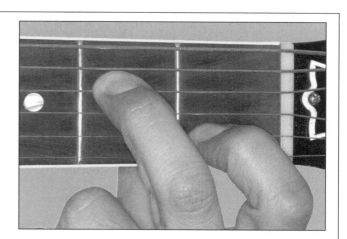

Dm7

Finally, we have Dm7. The curved line on top of the second and first strings on the chord box means you should let your first finger lie across the two strings at the first fret—this is called a *bar* (we'll examine this technique later on).

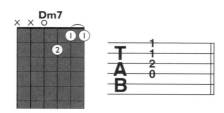

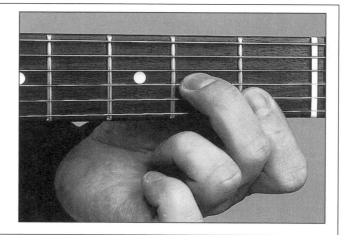

Minor 7th Chords

Bass–Chord Strumming

Here, we'll introduce a new playing technique along with these new chords called *bass–chord strumming*. This is where you combine playing just the lowest note from a chord (the *bass* note) with strumming the full chord.

Now try this light Spanish-style tune to test your bass–chord strumming and minor 7th chords. Listen to this tune being played on **Track 32** and try it yourself with **Track 33**.

Tracks 32 & 33

Now we go from very "sad" minor 7th chords to extremely "happy" *major 7th* chords, all of which are nice and easy to play.

Major 7th chords contain the seventh note of the major scale, which is one fret below the octave of the root. Compare the sounds of the following major 7th chords with their major triads.

Amaj7

First, let's try Amaj7. This chord uses the same shape and fingering as D7, just moved one set of strings over.

Compare the sound of a basic A major with this Amaj7 chord:

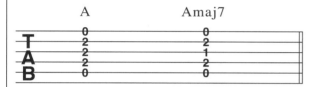

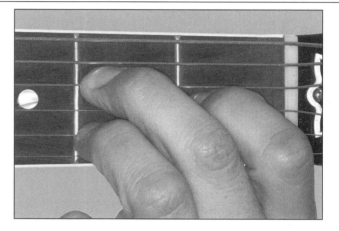

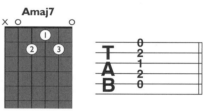

Cmaj7

Now for Cmaj7—only two fingers required for this one. The chord shape is actually very similar to G major but without having to make that finger-busting stretch.

Compare the sound of a basic C major with this Cmaj7 chord:

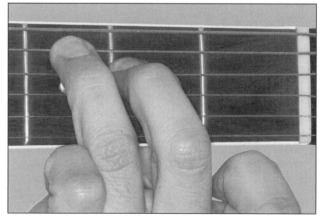

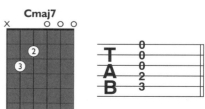

Dmaj7

This next one, Dmaj7, is an interesting one. There are two ways you could play this—either use fingers 1, 2, and 3, or simply lay your first finger across all three strings, as shown!

Compare the sound of a basic D major with this Dmaj7 chord:

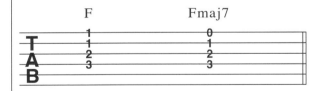

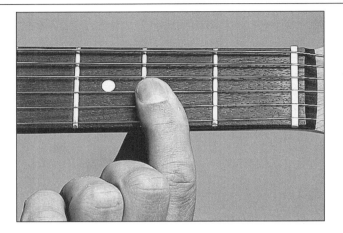

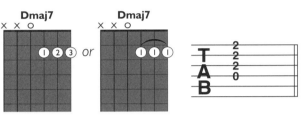

Fmaj7

Finally, we have Fmaj7. This is the first of the F chords so far, and certainly the easiest one to play that you'll encounter (for reasons you'll discover later on in the book). Careful with the fingering here as there's quite a lot of potential for buzzing across the top three strings.

Compare the sound of a basic F major with this Fmaj7 chord:

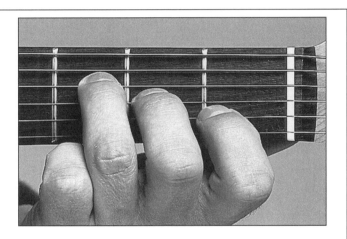

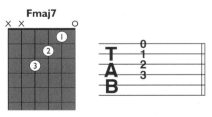

We'll try playing these chords as arpeggios rather than strumming them, picking each note out individually in this slow § tune.

Use upstrokes and downstrokes as indicated in the music, allowing the notes to ring out for the duration of the chord.

Tracks 34  35

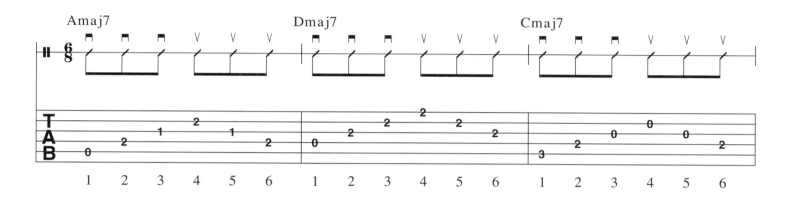

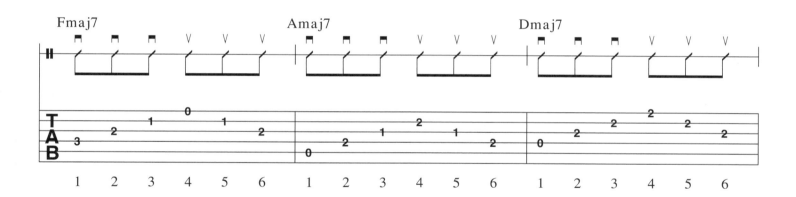

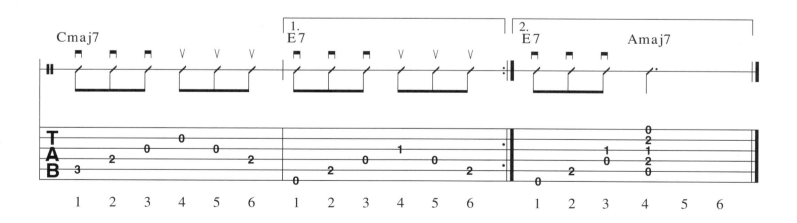

You can enhance the sound of bass–chord strumming by combining it with another commonly used guitar performance technique: the *hammer-on.* This is where the right hand picks a string and the left hand "hammers" a finger down onto a higher fret on that same string immediately afterwards, producing a second note from the continuing vibration of the string.

You can use hammer-ons in all types of ways—from making chord strumming more interesting to adding super-fast twiddly bits to guitar solos. (More to come on soloing later.)

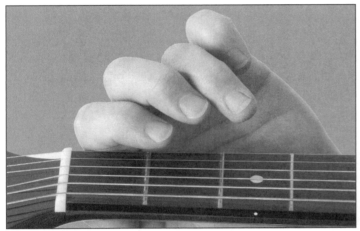

Step 1—The right hand picks the string

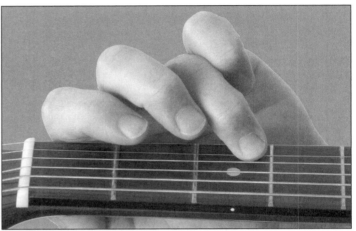

Step 2—THEN the left-hand finger hammers onto a higher fret

A hammer-on is written with a curved line (known as a *slur*) going from the lower (picked) note to the higher (hammered) note. The slur looks exactly like a tie but appears in both the rhythm staff AND the TAB staff, with an "H" written between the staves.

This first exercise should get you used to playing hammer-ons from a picked open string. Use your first finger on your left hand to hammer onto the first fret, the second finger to hammer the second fret, and so on. This is good practice for toughening up your little fourth finger! Listen to this exercise being played on **Track 36.**

Track (36)

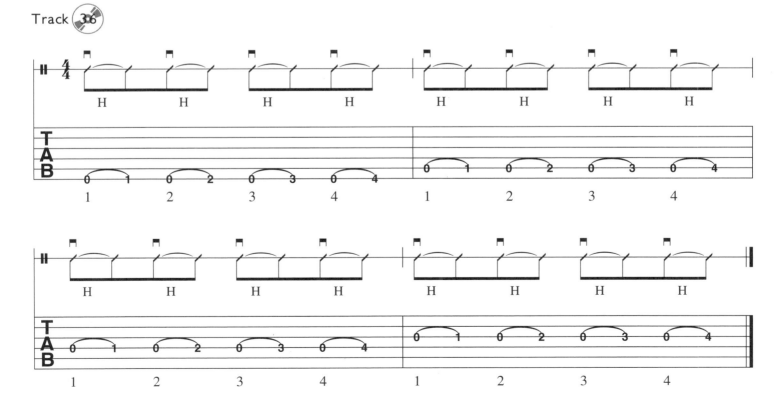

Now for the same sort of thing, but over three strings. Use your third finger to hammer onto the thick E string (sixth string), and your second finger on the A string (fifth string) and D string (fourth string).

Check out this exercise on **Track 37**. Bear in mind when practicing these exercises that you're going for accuracy and clarity of sound rather than high-speed hammer-ons—we'll do that later on in the book!

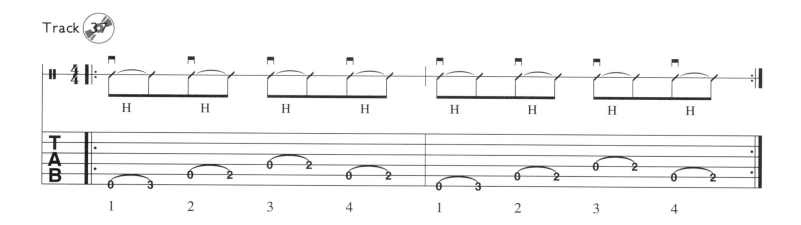

The Hammer-On

We've got another twelve-bar blues for you now, this time with a country/folk feel to it, and the object of this exercise is to play around on different strings within the chord rather than just strumming the whole thing—much easier than it sounds!

The bass–chord strumming style is expanded into picking and doing hammer-ons with other low notes from the chords (sometimes called *bass runs*), all of which can be achieved without moving your left hand away from the three basic chord shapes used. Accuracy with your right hand is absolutely essential here. Have a listen to this tune being played on **Track 38**, and then try it yourself along with **Track 39**.

Tracks 38  39

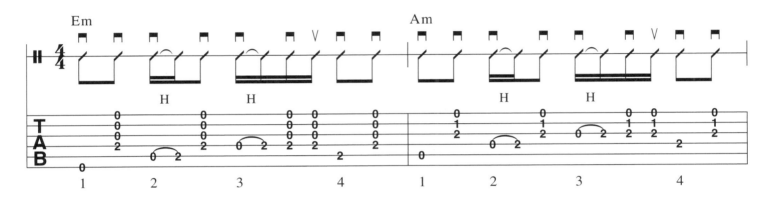

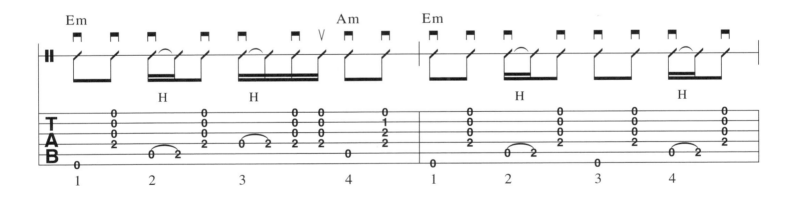

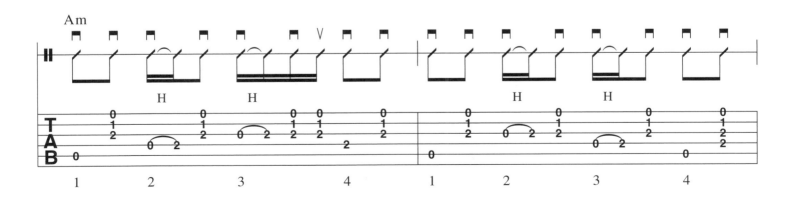

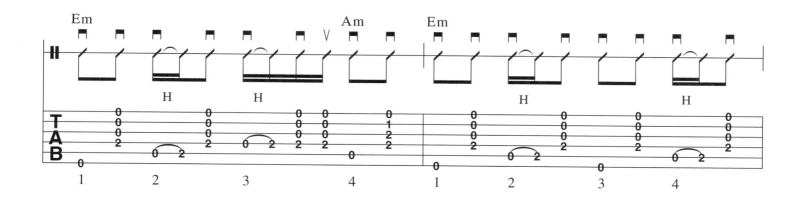

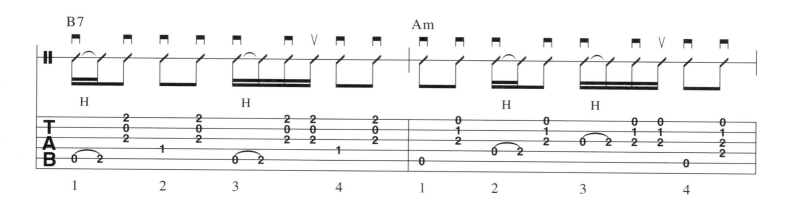

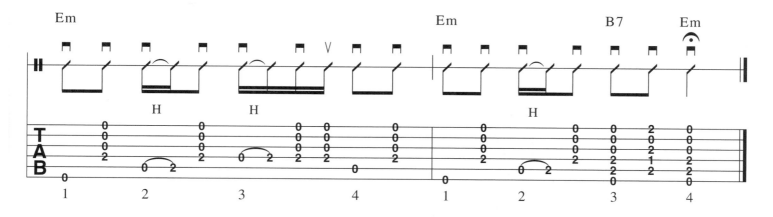

Playing Tip!
Once you've got this tune completely nailed (and don't cheat here), you can try making it a bit messy by "accidentally" strumming over more strings than written—it'll still sound cool, but more authentically folksy!

Fret Markers

The dots on the neck are there to help you find the correct frets more easily. There are normally fret markers at frets 3, 5, 7, 9, 12, 15, 17, 19, and 21 (and on fret 24 if your guitar neck goes that high).

The 12th fret usually has two dots to make it easier still. Get used to finding your way around the fretboard because we're about to start moving up the neck!

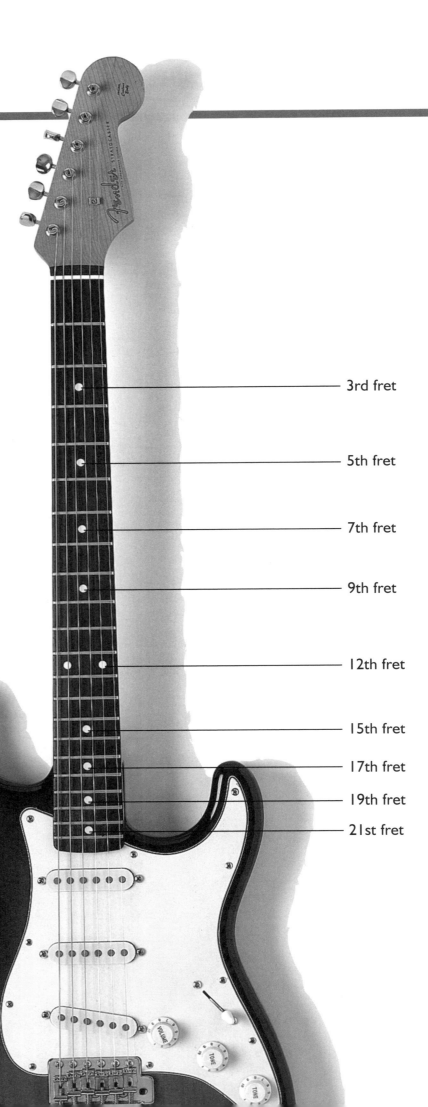

3rd fret

5th fret

7th fret

9th fret

12th fret

15th fret

17th fret

19th fret

21st fret

Every chord you've tried so far has been played right at the bottom of the neck and has used at least one open string, but the chord shapes we're about to look at can be moved anywhere on the fretboard. They involve holding down more than one string with the same finger, using that finger as a kind of "bar" across the fretboard. Therefore, these moveable chords are known as *bar chords*.

Bar chords tend to require more physical strain to play than any chord we've covered so far, but just remember that each new moveable bar-chord shape you learn will add twelve new chords to your collection (one on each fret up to the octave—or from E all the way up to E again), definitely making it worth putting in the practice.

We'll begin with the two most common major bar chords played right at the bottom of the neck (at the first fret).

F Major

First up is F major. This is basically the E major chord moved up one fret. Your first finger takes on the role of the nut and holds down (or bars) all the open strings at the first fret while your other three fingers form the chord shape above it.

Holding this chord down will take a fair amount of pressure from all your fingers in order to produce a clear, buzz-free sound, particularly on the thin E string, B string, and thick E string (first, second, and sixth strings), which are all barred by your first finger. Having your first finger in this position naturally weakens the strength of your other three fingers too, and getting used to accurately forming this chord shape in the first place will also feel a bit tricky—it's worth laying each finger down carefully, one at a time, while you get used to it.

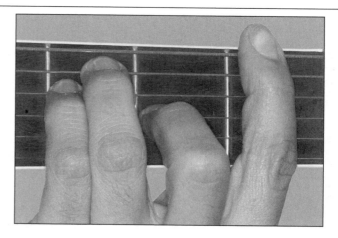

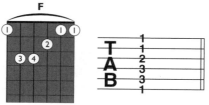

Before you let any of this dishearten you, it's worth remembering that there are professional guitarists playing throughout the world who find the F major chord difficult and annoying to play even after years of practice and performance!

It's quite simply a very unnatural position in which to hold your fingers, and doesn't feel any less weird even when you move the entire shape up the neck (although it will be easier to hold the strings down the higher up you go). Many guitarists have even been known to retune their instruments completely just to avoid having to play the F major chord shape (Joni Mitchell, for example).

So don't be scared by the "daddy" of all bar chords—practice is the key here, and there's no better chord for toughening up your fingers than F major. Get this one under your belt and you'll already be ahead of some of the most famous guitarists ever!

B♭ Major

And now for B♭ major. A similar situation to before, this is basically the A major chord moved up one fret, with your first finger taking on the role of the nut and barring the first fret and your other three fingers forming the chord shape above it. Remember to avoid strumming the thick E string (sixth string).

Your fingers will seem even more bunched up here than when you were playing the F major chord, and it's worth trying to form the chord shape one finger at a time as we did before. Getting your second, third, and fourth fingers aligned so tightly behind the first finger can seem a clumsy business at first, especially since the position of the first finger will once again weaken the strength of the others. Most potential buzzing or accidental muting of this chord will be caused by insufficient finger pressure on the strings. If you hear any problems, pick through the chord string by string until you identify where the trouble is coming from.

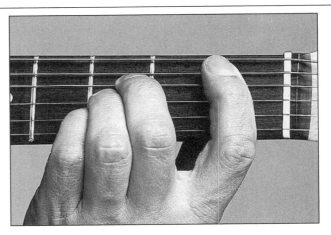

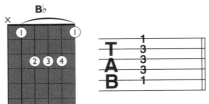

B♭ Major (cheater's version)

Some people find B♭ major even harder to get to grips with than F major (including the author of this book—I hate it!) but, once again, practice is the key! There are so many tunes that can be played with this chord shape that it's definitely worth taking the time to master it. However, if you happen to be REALLY impatient, then there is the "cheater's" method of playing B♭ major.

Four strings barred with two fingers, involving possibly more finger pressure than the standard method of playing B♭ major! This chord requires extreme strumming precision, as you're only playing the four "inside" strings of the guitar, leaving out the top and bottom E strings (first and sixth strings), and places the bulk of the left-hand stress on the third finger rather than the first. But who cares—it's an incredibly easy chord shape to form and there's very little chance for buzzing to happen anywhere. So, it's entirely up to you whether you want to use the "correct" version or the cheater's method.

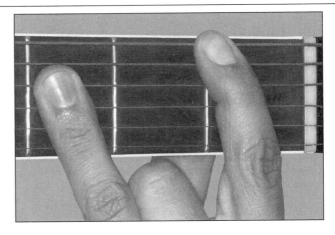

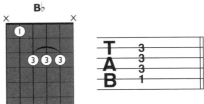

Here's a slow, gentle tune in ¾ to try out your F and B♭ major chords, which should help you get used to jumping between open chords and bar chords. The full B♭ chord has been used in the TAB, but (as with any other tune in this book) feel free to use the cheater's version if you prefer.

We'll include some simple bass–chord strumming here too— remember to take it nice and easy. Listen to this tune being played on **Track 40** and try it yourself with **Track 41**.

Tracks 40 & 41

G Major

The next logical step with using moveable chords is to try, well, moving them! Taking our F major chord shape and shifting it up the neck by two frets gives us this new way of playing G major. Your first-finger bar should now be at the third fret.

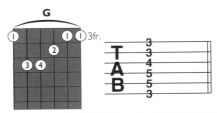

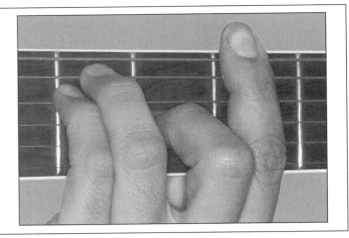

C Major

And if you try the same two-fret move with the B♭ chord shape (full or cheater's version), you end up with this new way of playing C major. (You can let your first finger hang over onto the bottom string to mute it.)

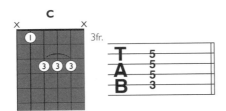

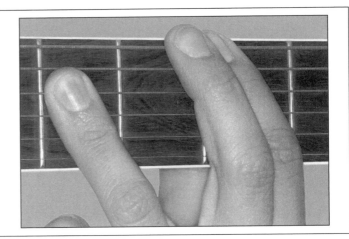

Try going back and forth between G and C in this little chord progression:

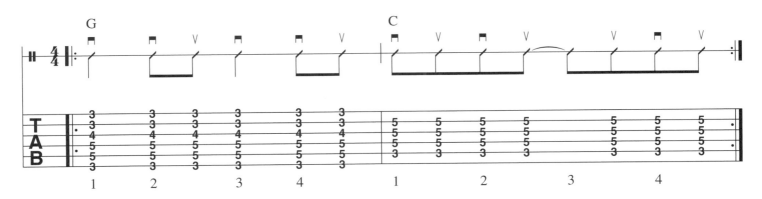

So with just two different chord shapes we can produce a four-chord tune like this. Finger-busting stuff, but VERY good practice! Listen to this tune on **Track 42** and try it yourself with **Track 43**.

Here are some big chord frames to help you memorize the shapes and positions for this next tune.

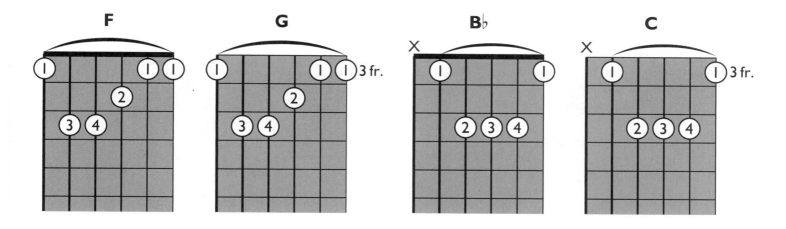

Tracks 42  43

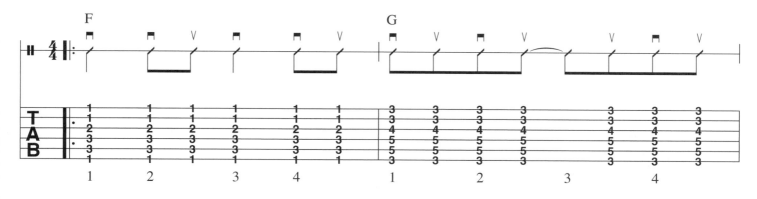

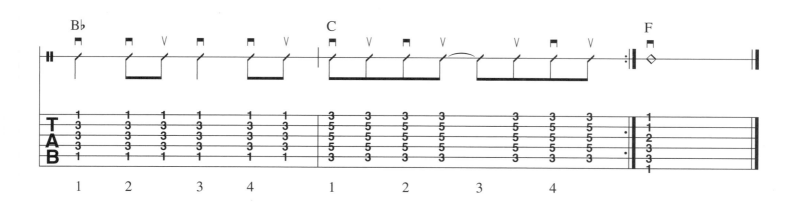

Time to have a look at three variations of your F major chord shape, all of which, like F major, are E chord shapes moved up a fret.

Once you have the trick of playing the basic F chord shape, it's simple to form these others, since all they require is for you to remove fingers from the fretboard (again, exactly the same way as the different E chords).

F7

We'll start with F7—it's just an F major chord with the little finger removed, although be careful that your second and third fingers don't catch the B and D strings (second and fourth strings) and cause muting or buzzing.

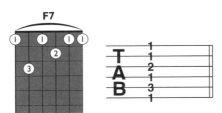

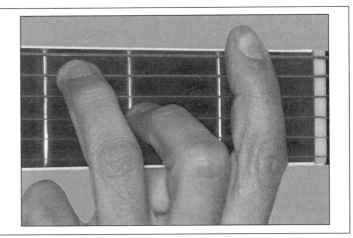

F Minor

F minor is easier still—it's the F major chord with the second finger taken away, which you'll probably find a bit easier to play without buzzing.

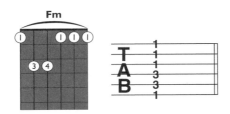

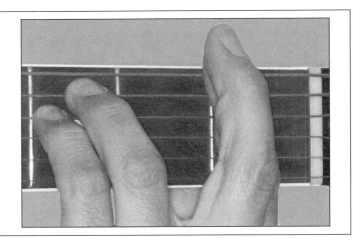

Fm7

Finally, we have a really simple shape for Fm7—one finger holding the bar and only one other finger holding a string down. A very easy chord to form!

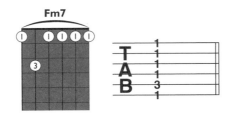

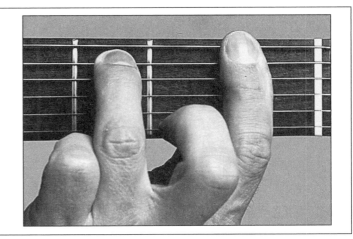

Try this short exercise to practice changing between the chord shapes. It's a bit of a tongue-twister, in terms of "basic" chords (called *triads*) versus 7th chords, but you get to keep your hand in the same place and strum ALL the strings (so it's not *that* much of a chore!).

Here are some big chord frames to help you memorize the shapes and positions.

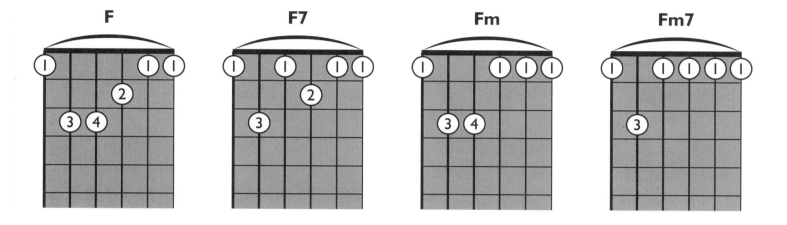

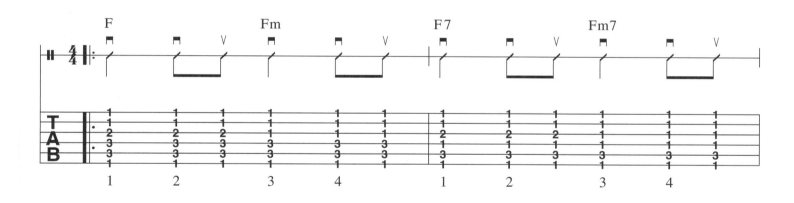

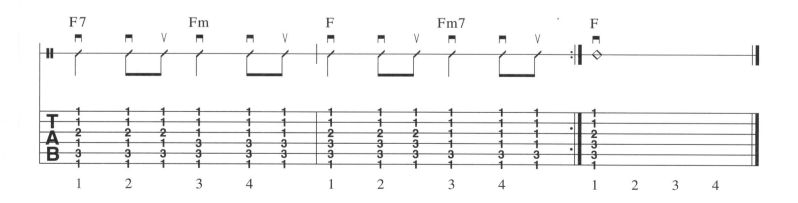

Roots on the 6th String

This chart shows you the names of all the notes found on the thick E string (sixth string), all of which can provide the root (the bass note with the same name as the chord) for F-shaped bar chords played up and down the neck.

Get used to forming the four different shapes we've looked at and you can use them to form chords based on all these notes. It really is THAT simple!

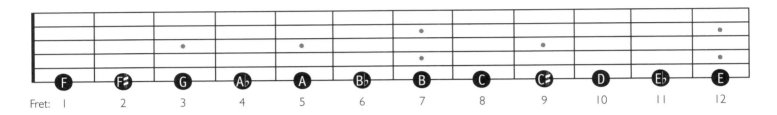

Fret: 1 2 3 4 5 6 7 8 9 10 11 12

Here's a four-bar pattern with a few rests thrown in, using the different F chord shapes to play some completely new chords.

We've included mini chord boxes that show you which fret to bar. Check out this tune on **Track 44** and then play along with **Track 45**.

Tracks 44 & 45

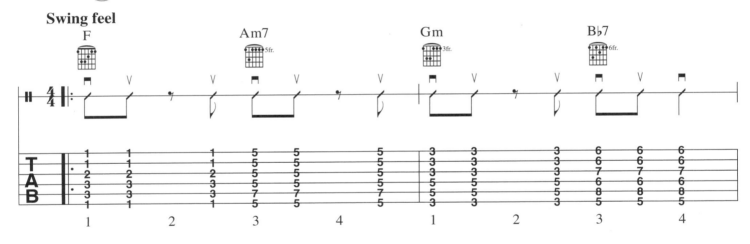

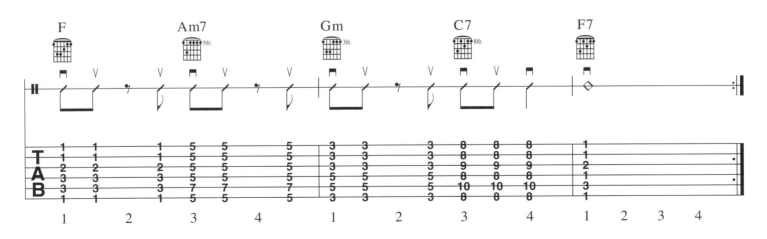

Incredible! Without even realizing it, you have now learned the "standard" way of playing a G minor chord.

Try strumming between C major and G minor if you've got a moment, as it sounds rather nice and is a very good chord change to practice.

The variations of the B♭-shaped bar chord are a little trickier than the F shapes, especially since there are no "cheats" for you to fall back on (unlike the B♭ major chord), but they're just as useful in terms of opening up lots of new chords for you to play.

Think of them as variations of the A chord moved up a fret with the first finger providing the bar, and remember to leave out the thick E string (sixth string) when you strum.

B♭7

First, we'll try B♭7. Lots of potential buzzes here, so be careful when positioning your third and fourth fingers.

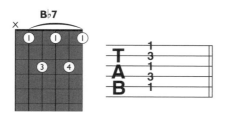

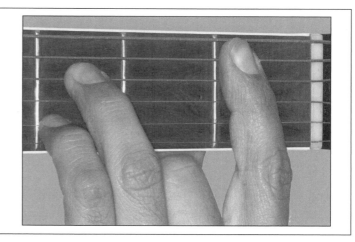

B♭ Minor

Now for B♭ minor. This is almost identical to playing the F major chord—just move the entire shape down!

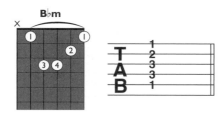

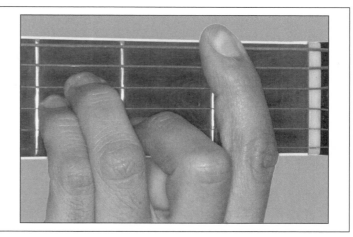

B♭m7

Last of all, we have B♭m7. Uncanny—this one is almost identical to playing the F7 chord, with the entire shape moved over a string again. Ah, if only all new chords were this easy!

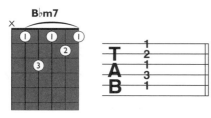

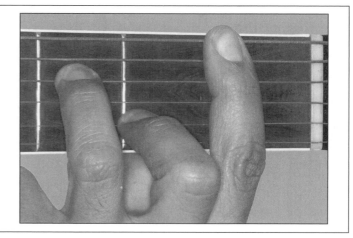

Variations on B♭: B♭7, B♭m, and B♭m7

Here are some big chord frames to help you memorize the shapes and positions for this next tune.

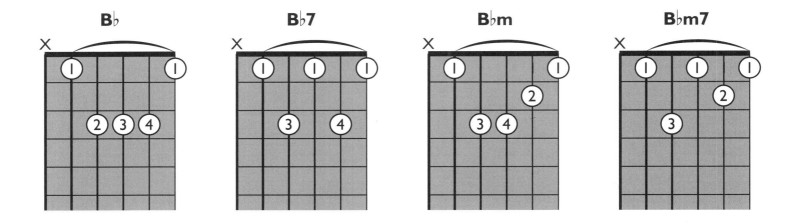

This next exercise gives you practice at jumping between the various B♭ chord shapes AND at jumping between similar F and B♭ chord shapes.

You should keep your first finger barred across all strings at the first fret throughout.

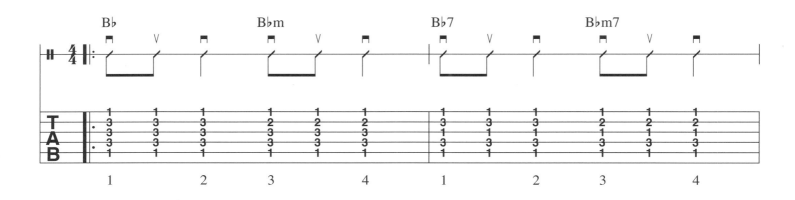

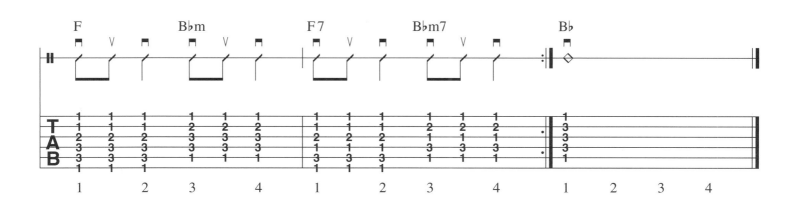

Roots on the 5th String

Here's another picture of the neck, this time showing you the names of the notes found on the A string (fifth string), all of which can provide roots for B♭-shaped bar chords played up and down the neck.

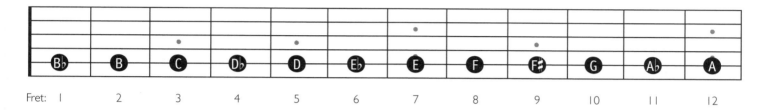

We'll use our B♭ chord shapes mixed with F chord shapes and a swing rhythm for this exercise (along with the mini chord boxes again to make things easier).

Don't forget to play the 1st and 2nd time endings! Have a listen to this exercise being played on **Track 46** and try it yourself with **Track 47.**

Tracks 46  47

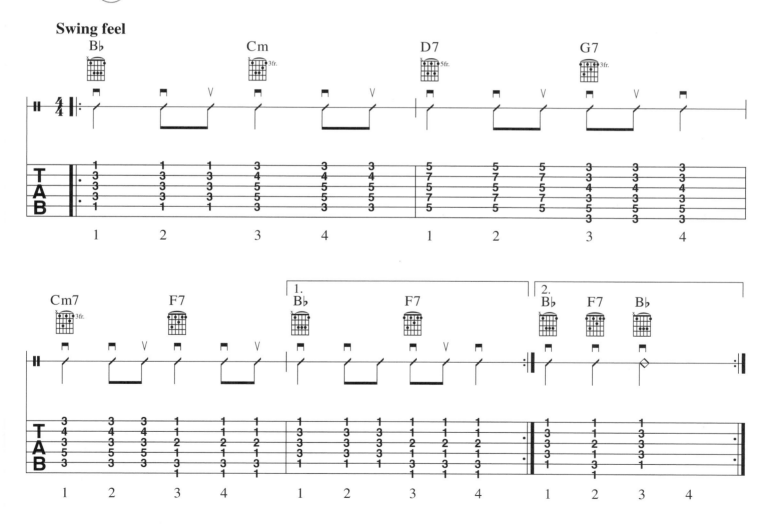

And that's another three "standard" chords for your collection: Cm, Cm7, and G7, all of which are simple bar chords.

Again, strumming between the Cm7 and G7 chords is another nice chord change (almost a Latin feel—try it and see).

C9

Now for a chord shape that was designed to be seriously cool: the *9th* chord, which is used extensively in jazz and funk music. Try this C9 chord:

Here we have the third finger acting as the bar, and it's only holding down three strings rather than providing the root and entire foundation of the chord. Your first and second fingers are making up the rest of the shape on the two strings below the bar, and you'll find that the whole shape can be held down firmly with less strain than all previous bar chords. This makes it easier for you to slide the chord up and down the fretboard, which is great news, since the 9th chord is at it's best when slipping all over the place! Be sure to leave out the thick E string (sixth string) when you strum.

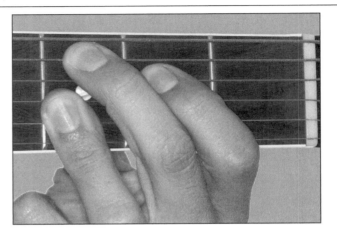

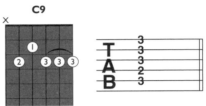

We'll now move the 9th chord up to the sixth and seventh frets (giving us E♭9 and E9) for the next tune.

E♭9

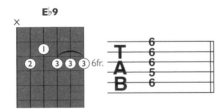

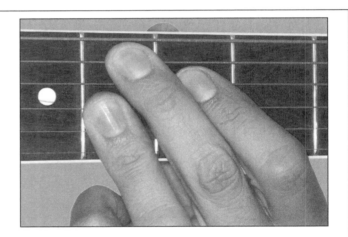

E9

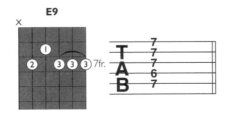

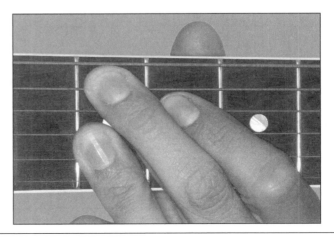

Left-Hand Muting

The perfect accompaniment for playing funky 9th chords is a technique called *left-hand muting*, where you hold your fretting hand over the strings to deaden the notes completely and strum them lightly with the pick. A mute is written as an **X** in both the rhythm and TAB staves, and you can position your left hand anywhere on the neck as you mute it (although it's sensible to keep it near the frets that you've just played or are about to play!).

For the next tune we'll use our 9th chords, left-hand muting, and throw in some extremely funky rhythms!

Make sure you keep those staccato notes nice and tight. Check out **Track 48** and then play along with **Track 49.**

This is the point at which many guitarists decide they never want to play anything other than funk ever again.

Tracks 48 & 49

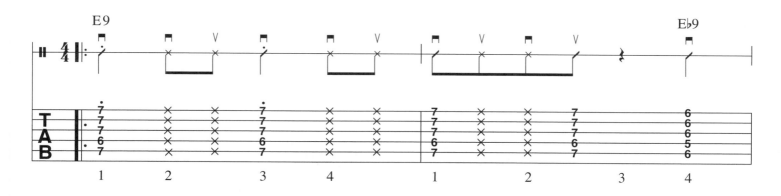

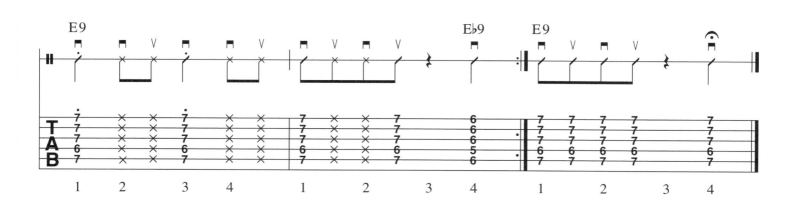

Now for some more fun. These two chord shapes are half-bars, or "mini" versions of the F-shaped major and minor bar chords, using only the top four strings of each chord.

Remember that for both these "mini" chords, you'll need to avoid strumming the A string and thick E string (fifth and sixth strings).

F Major Half-Bar

First, a mini F major. The first finger is providing the bar again, but holding down only two strings, which should feel a LOT easier than the "big" F major chord.

Practice strumming mini F in the following pattern:

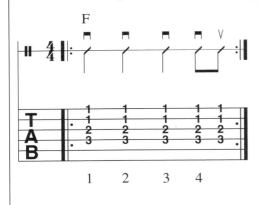

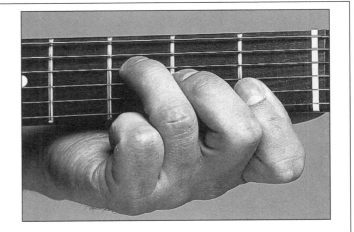

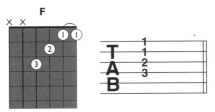

A Minor Half-Bar

Here's a similar situation with this mini A minor. Only two fingers required—if only all our chords could be played like this!

Practice strumming mini Am in the following pattern:

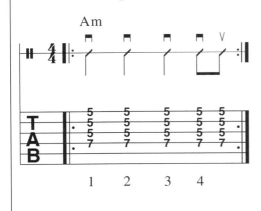

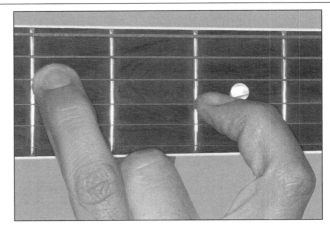

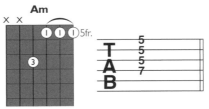

You're now going to do a Bob Marley impersonation and play a little reggae, a style distinctive for the way you play the chords on the off beats in each bar—just tap your foot along to the beat and strum between taps! We'll slide the major chord shape up two frets and start on G for this one.

Yet again, you'll need to keep the staccato notes nice and tight, and don't let the bass drum on the track throw you off (reggae drummers hit the bass drum on beats 2 and 4 rather than on beats 1 and 3). Listen to **Track 50** and then try it yourself with **Track 51**.

Tracks 50 & 51

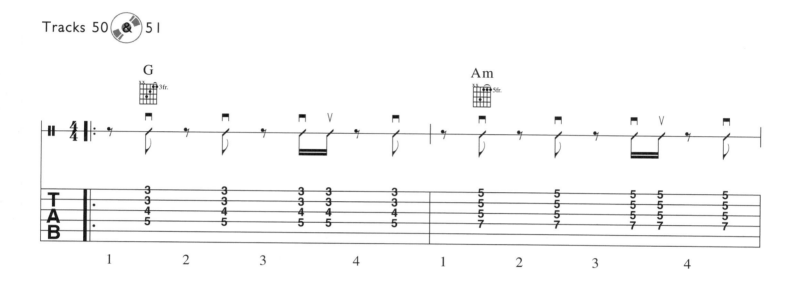

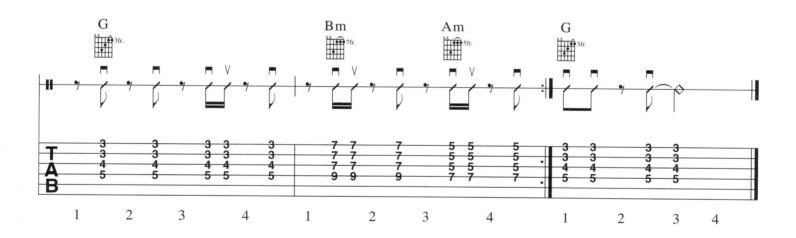

Very chilled out—try to grow your hair in dreadlocks for added authenticity.

Power chords (or *5th* chords) form the basis of most rock music, nearly all heavy metal, and a great deal of rock 'n' roll, and their incredible simplicity makes them great fun to play.

They're made up of two notes (the root and the fifth) and can be played with either two or three strings—it doesn't really make much difference since the third string just plays another root note an octave higher.

Open Power Chords

We'll start with three power chords at the bottom of the neck, using the three-stringed versions of each chord.

E5

First, we have E5. Not much to go wrong here, so long as you remember you're only playing the bottom three strings.

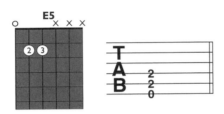

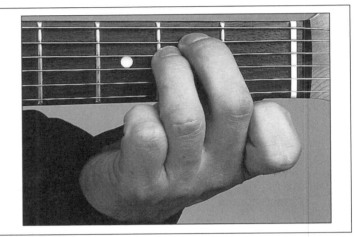

A5

Here's the A5 chord, which is exactly the same shape but shifted over a set of strings.

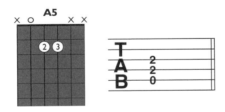

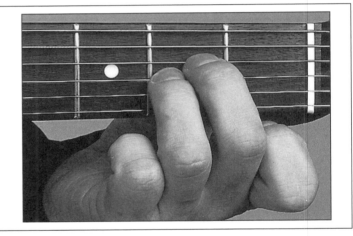

D5

Now for D5. There's a slightly different fingering here, and you obviously can't get away with barring this chord. Just imagine it's a D major without the top note.

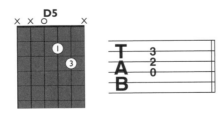

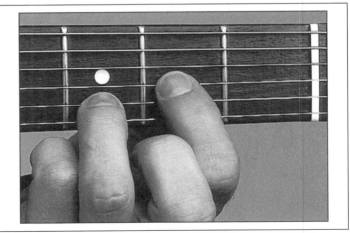

Power Chords

Pay particular attention to the strum markings for this tune, since the individual notes are all played with downstrokes, and accurately strumming power chords up and down takes a fair bit of precision.

Listen to this being played on **Track 52** and play along with **Track 53**.

Tracks 52 & 53

Classic Blues Riff

Now let's go from rock to blues, playing the two-note versions of E5 and A5 and expanding them into 6ths and 7ths here and there, along with a few more extra notes and a swing feel in the rhythm. This is *the* classic blues pattern, or *riff*. This might sound like a bit of a confusing leap from plain power chords, but it's actually quite simple to play.

Keep your first finger hovering around the second fret (with your other three fingers over the next three frets) and you'll find you don't have to move your left hand at all! Note the downstrokes throughout, giving it a more "raw" blues sound. Check out **Track 54** and try it yourself with **Track 55**.

Tracks 54 & 55

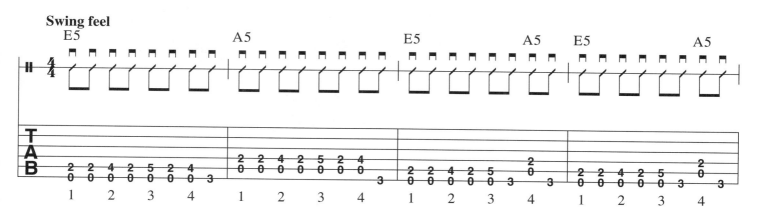

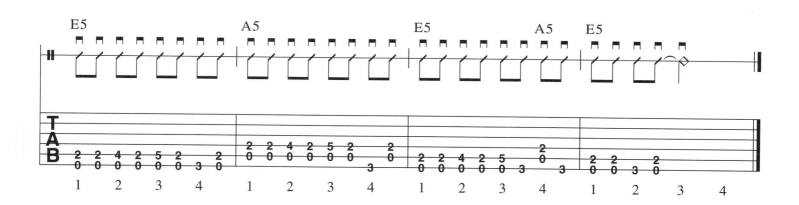

Power Chords

Moveable Power Chords on the 6th and 5th Strings

Moveable power chords are where the fun really begins, since you can easily form them pretty much anywhere up and down the neck, giving you a simple way of playing just about any tune imaginable.

Once again, you can use either two or three strings, and the chord shapes are identical.

G5

We'll start on the low E string at the third fret, playing a G5.

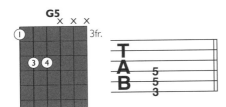

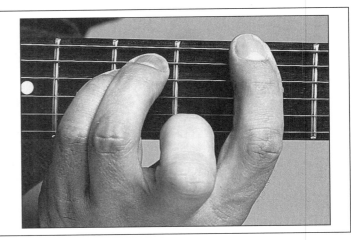

C5

Now move the shape over to the A string to make a C5.

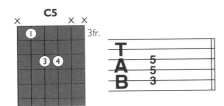

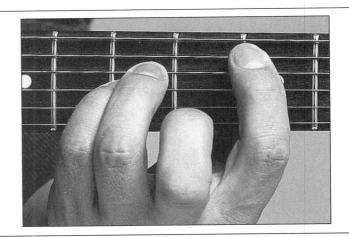

The fingering is identical for either chord position, but you can cheat here again by barring the top two notes if you want.

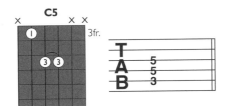

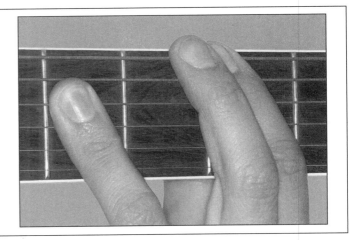

Palm Mute and Accents

A commonly used technique when playing rock tunes with power chords is the *palm mute*—this is where the palm of your right hand rests lightly against the strings at the bridge while you strum (usually with downstrokes), damping the sound slightly.

Palm-muted notes are indicated with P.M. ------- ┤, with a line extending from the "P.M." to cover any following notes that are to be muted in the same way.

We'll also *accent* some of the chords in this tune. Strum extra hard whenever you see a ⤋ symbol to make them stand out a bit more than the others.

Let's try another rock tune—more of an 80s feel to this one!

Notice that the same B♭ power chord appears in two different places on the neck during this tune—the same is possible with all other power chords (some can even be played in three or four different spots).

In this case, it's simply easier to jump from the E♭5 to the B♭5 in the eighth measure by moving the entire chord shape over one set of strings rather than shifting it down five frets on the same strings.

Listen to **Track 56** and then try it yourself with **Track 57.**

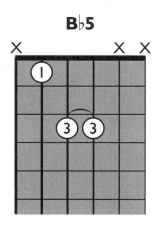

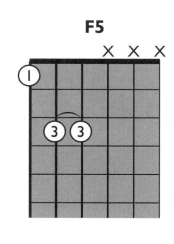

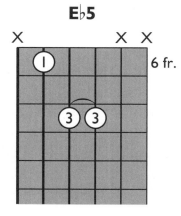

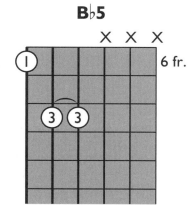

Power Chords

Tracks 56 & 57

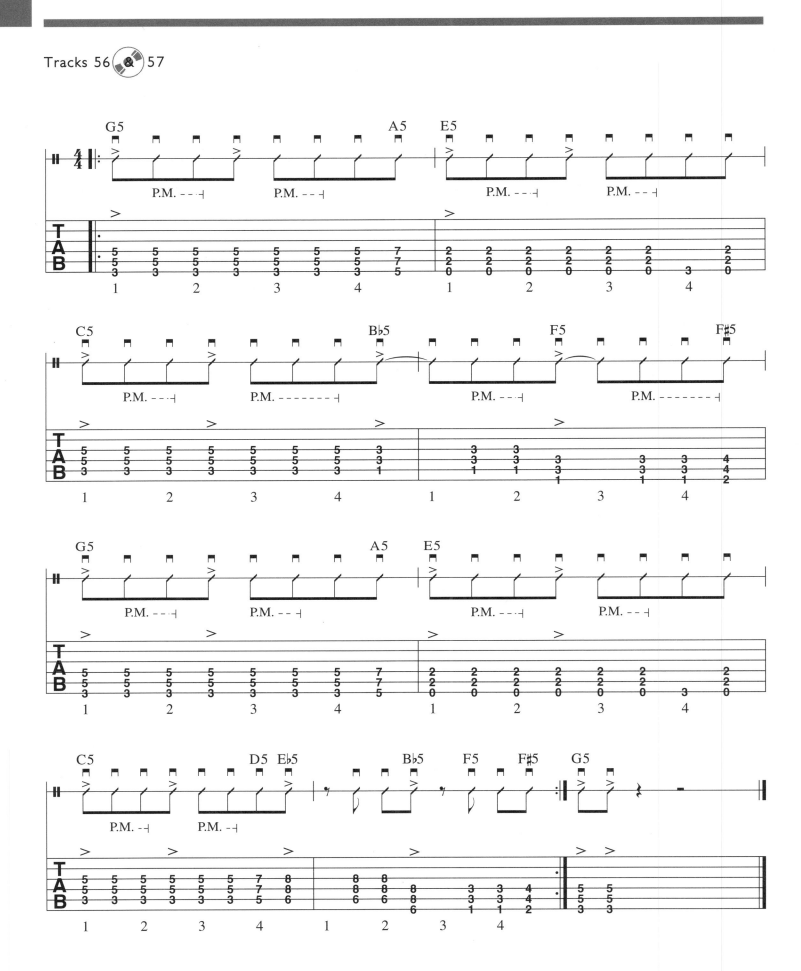

Now it's time to lay down your pick for the moment and play *fingerstyle*. To be more specific, you're going to pluck the strings individually with the thumb and first three fingers of your right hand rather than strum them.

The term "fingerstyle" actually covers quite a wide variety of different fingerpicking techniques—claw picking, Travis picking, Carter solos, arpeggio style, the list goes on and on, but they all generally rely on the same principles. The thumb is mainly used to pluck the lower strings (the fourth, fifth, and sixth strings) while the first, second, and third fingers cover the higher strings. The fourth finger is rarely used in fingerstyle playing.

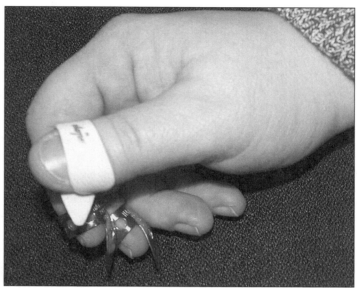

Some guitarists use fingerpicks and thumbpicks—plastic or metal devices worn on the fingers and thumb. These can give a clearer tone when picking but are tricky to use.

We'll use these letters above the TAB staff to indicate which right-hand fingers you should be using to pick which strings:

T	=	Thumb
I	=	Index finger
M	=	Middle finger
R	=	Ring finger

Your right hand should be positioned over the strings with your thumb away from your fingers. Keep your hand slightly cupped and the wrist slightly raised, as in the photo above. The aim here should be to let your fingers and thumb do the work, rather than plucking the strings by moving your whole hand up and down. The strings should be plucked using the side of your thumb and the fleshy tips of your fingers, unless you have long fingernails and prefer using those instead!

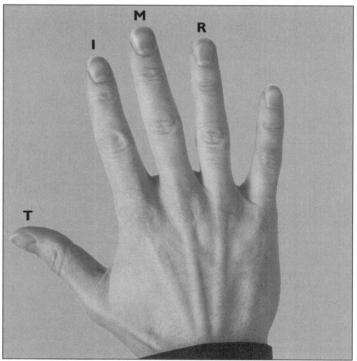

And remember: When playing fingerstyle you should ONLY pluck what's written in the TAB—don't strum anything else!

Claw Picking

Here's a very basic *claw picking* exercise on A major to get you started.

It's so called because you use all three fingers to pluck the strings at the same time, making a "claw" shape with your hand.

A general rule of fingerstyle is that you should allow the plucked strings to ring throughout the duration of the chord you're picking, or at least until you come to a rest. This makes the whole chord sound richer and gives you fewer worries about having to mute strings all over the place.

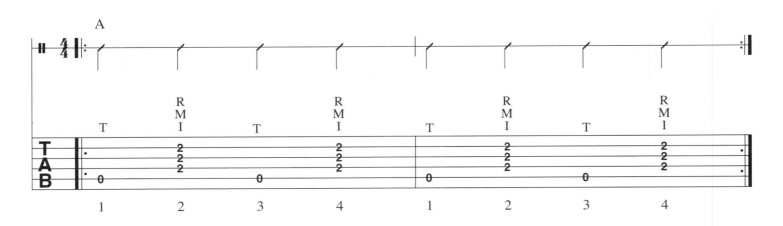

This next tune is a jazz piece with a swing feel (so don't forget to give it some bounce), and uses simple claw picking, but with a few more chords. Note that the final chord is played with a standard downstroke—do this with the backs of your fingernails.

Once you've got the hang of claw picking this tune, you could try playing it *thumb–brush* style: pick the bass notes with your thumb and lightly downstrum the rest of the chords with your fingernails. Listen to **Track 58** and then give it a try yourself with **Track 59.**

Tracks 58  59

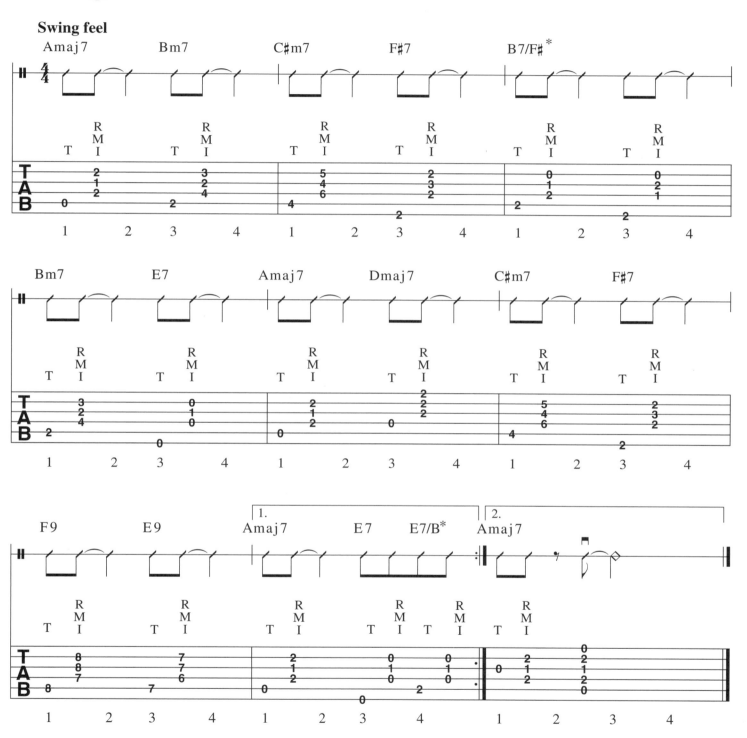

* These two chords are played over *alternate bass notes*—the chord symbol is followed by a forward slash and the new bass note. The first example would be described as "B7 over F♯" (simply move the 2nd finger of your left hand over a string to play this) and the second as "E7 over B." Alternate bass notes are fairly common in fingerstyle guitar music.

Fingerstyle Arpeggios

Playing an *arpeggio* (or *broken chord*, as it's also known) is just as easy in fingerstyle as it is with a pick. Here is an accompanying guitar line for the traditional English folk song "Scarborough Fair" for you to try.

Again, remember to let the individual notes ring out for the length of each chord. Listen to this tune being played on **Track 60** and try it yourself with **Track 61**.

SCARBOROUGH FAIR

Tracks 60 & 61

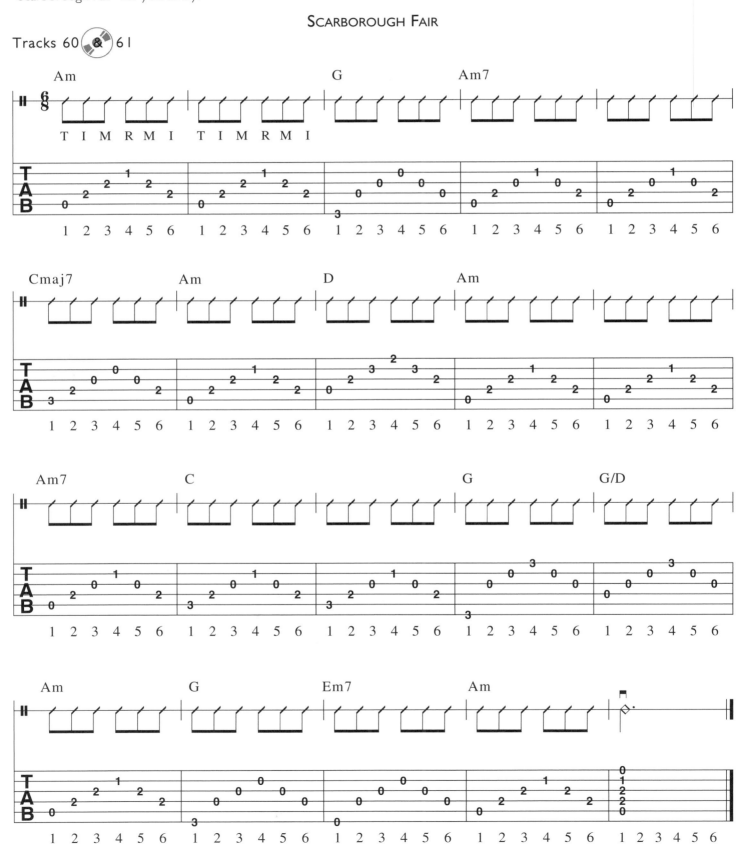

Here's a tune with some more extended broken chords.

Tracks 62 & 63

Travis Picking

Travis picking (named after country music legend Merle Travis) is the king of guitar fingerstyle playing—hugely popular, extremely versatile, and a little trickier to get the hang of than arpeggio style. But since you can use it to play folk, blues, country and much more, it's a very good technique to master, and it is also marvelous for impressing non-guitarists, who will be amazed you can carry it off without tying your fingers into huge knots.

In the exercise below we're going to build up to Travis picking one step at a time, ending up with an alternating bass note and rolling around the high notes of our B7 chord. Don't forget the repeats. Read through the four points to remember, take a deep breath, and go for it!

Four Points to Remember:

1. It's not as complicated as it looks.
2. Your thumb always plays on the beat—usually every quarter note—and only picks the two or three bass strings in a chord.
3. Your index and middle fingers almost always play off the beat—usually between every quarter note—and pluck the higher strings in a chord. The ring finger is rarely used in Travis picking.
4. The first beat of a Travis-picked bar of music commonly involves the pinch, where the thumb and second finger pick the bass note and a higher note from the chord at the same time.

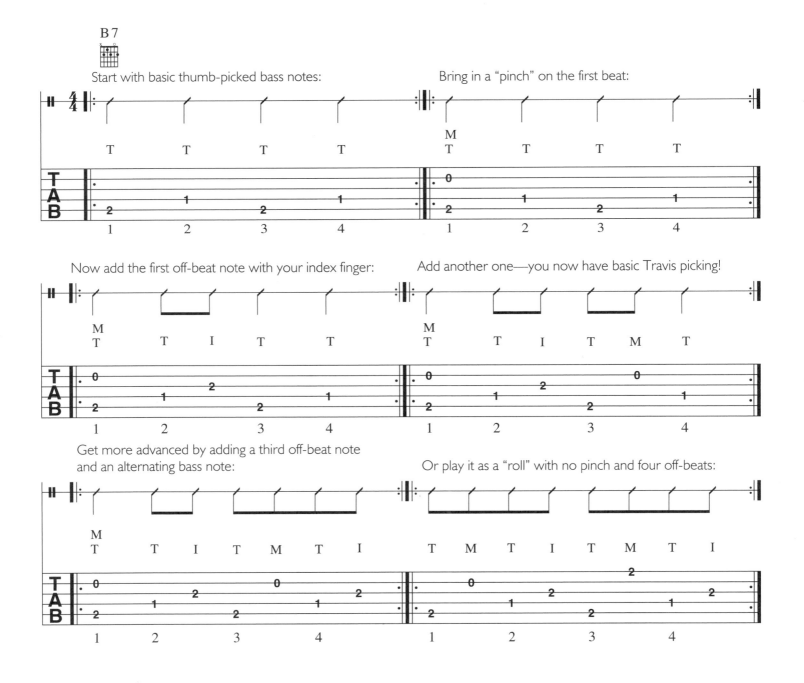

Now let's try it in a chord progression. Listen for rolls and alternating bass notes on **Track 64** and then try it yourself with **Track 65.**

Tracks 64 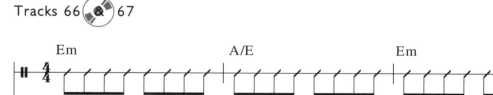 65

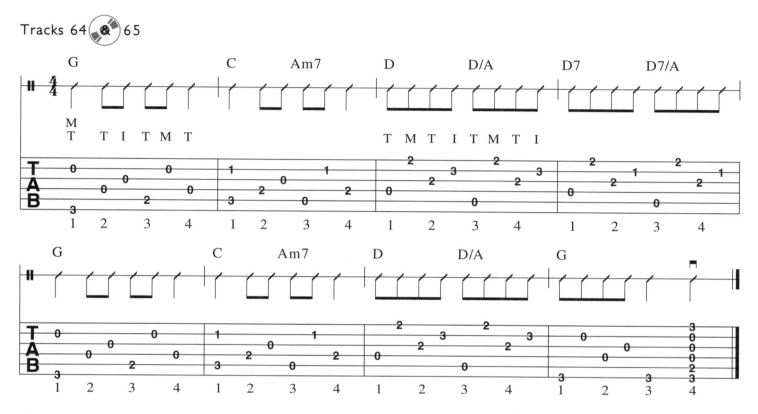

This next exercise is a little different and altogether "darker" sounding, with a constant E in the bass—this is known as a *pedal tone.*

Form the other chord shapes as normal above this pedal E. Listen to **Track 66** and the play along with **Track 67.**

Tracks 66 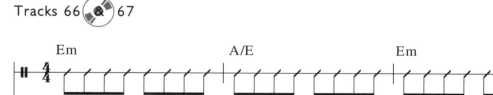 67

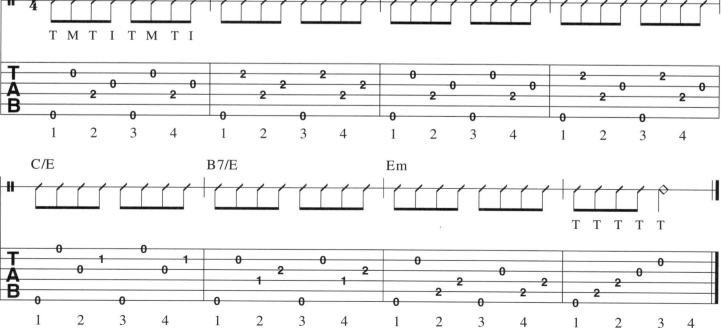

Lead Guitar

Playing lead guitar is a subject that you probably could not entirely fit into its own dedicated book (never mind a complete guitar method), as there is literally no limit to the styles, scales, speeds, tricks, tunings, and flashes of inspiration that a player can put into his or her 6-string melodies. Most guitarists make it up as they go along anyway, a habit which has turned out some of the most incredible and famous guitar solos in history.

For all we know the greatest guitar solo ever may not yet have been played—in fact it could even be you who, one day, records the lead guitar line that everyone will be humming and trying to play for eternity. If so, then congratulations (and don't forget to tell the world that this was the book that started you off).

Despite the sheer enormousness of what can be done with lead guitar playing, we CAN give you plenty of pointers to guide you in the right direction when it comes to playing one note at a time rather than strumming or picking chords.

The Basics

Keep your right arm and hand nicely relaxed, holding the pick normally but not TOO firmly—playing solos with either a pick or your fingers is much more difficult if you're tense.

Many guitarists like to anchor their right hand somewhere on the guitar in order to improve picking accuracy. This is normally done by resting a few fingers on the guitar body just below the strings or resting your palm on the bridge, being sure not to mute any strings while you're playing.

Endeavor to keep the fingers of your fretting hand AND the pick close to the strings even when they're not playing a note—many beginners try to keep their hands as far away from the strings as possible, making playing unnecessarily difficult.

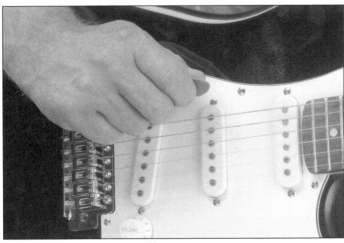

Wrong way

Right way

The majority of the melodies we're going to look at are all based around the first four frets, so make sure you're using ALL FOUR FINGERS on your left hand to play them—first finger on the first fret, second finger on the second fret, and so on. Too many beginners get into the bad habit of playing guitar solos with just their first and second fingers since they're naturally stronger, but your third and fourth fingers WILL strengthen with practice.

Other Points to Remember:

- Avoid pressing the strings down too hard against the frets. This can lead to you accidentally bending the strings and putting your notes out of tune. It also hurts!

- Hold the strings down right behind the fret when playing notes—it's easier on the fingers and the notes are less likely to buzz.

- When moving up from one note to another on the same string, do not remove the finger from the lower note until after you've fretted the higher note. Conversely, when moving down the notes on the same string, make sure you are already fretting the lower note before removing the finger from the higher note. Doing all this will make your playing sound much smoother (called *legato*).

Here's a short exercise to get you used to smooth fret changes on individual strings. Play this up-and-down pattern on all the strings of your guitar, as fast as you want, until you've got it sounding nice and buzz-free, paying careful attention to the upstrokes and downstrokes.

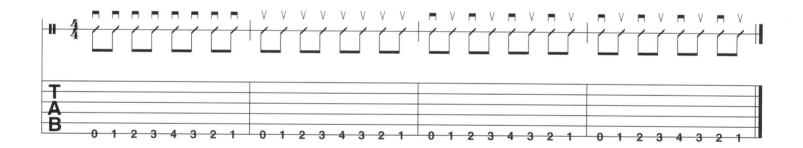

Did You Know?

Lead guitar melodies are generally based around the notes that make up the chord or key of the tune you're playing, all of which can be found in the scale of that key. A *scale* is defined as "an ascending or descending collection of pitches proceeding by and adhering to a specified scheme of intervals."

Or, more simply, it's a bunch of notes that you know will sound sweet when played over certain chords.

Lead Guitar

E Major Scale

We are going to start our lead guitar playing in E major, so let's first get acquainted with the E major scale. Here it is written in TAB—the notes in bold make up an E major chord.

When mixed with the other notes, they make up the *key of E major*. The accompanying scale box shows you which fingers to use.

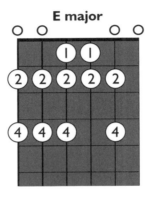

E major

| E | F# | G# | A | B | C# | D# | E | F# | G# | A | B | C# | D# | E |

This location at the bottom of the neck is called *first position,* where you involve open strings in your soloing and your four fingers stay on the four frets closest to the nut (first finger at the first fret, second finger at the second fret, etc.). The E major scale is a good way to start practicing moving up and down the notes and strings, forcing you to use your little finger, which should hopefully toughen it up nicely!

Now let's try a tune in E major, played with downstrokes throughout and featuring a few hammer-ons here and there.

Check out **Track 68** and then try it yourself with **Track 69.**

Tracks 68 & 69

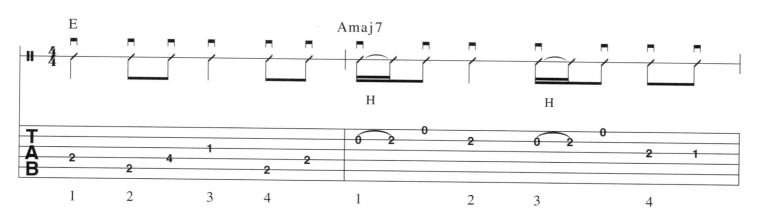

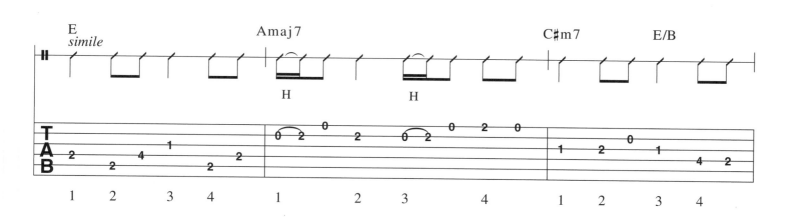

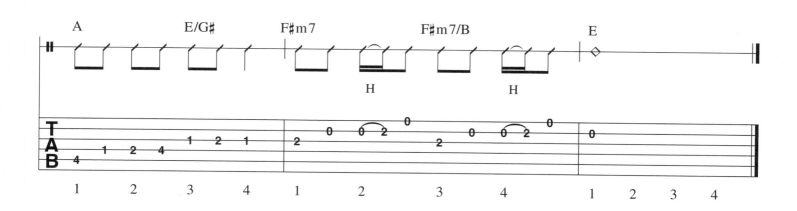

A Major Scale

Next up we have the A major scale, this time using ALL your fingers (note the shift to second position on the high E string).

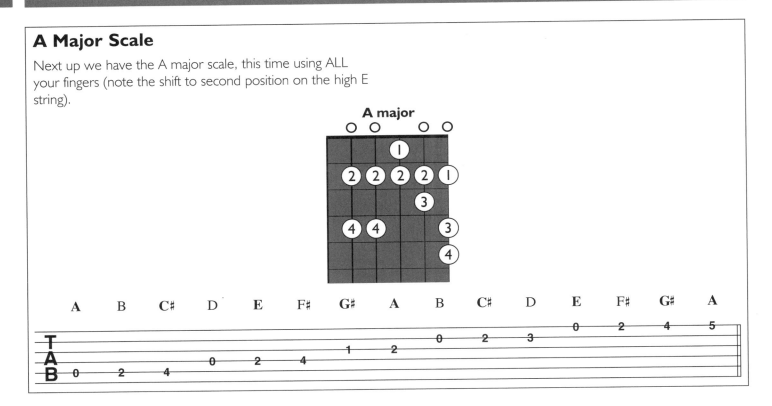

This A-major waltz is going to start speeding up your fingering and string changes, using upstrokes as well as downstrokes to make it a bit trickier.

It's not essential to always use a constant up/down motion with your pick when playing lead guitar (compared to when you're strumming chords), but it's good to practice picking in both directions to help your speed. Have a listen to **Track 70** and then try to play along with **Track 71**.

Tracks 70 & 71

A Minor Pentatonic

A *pentatonic* scale contains only five different notes, but it's amazing what you can do with just five notes!

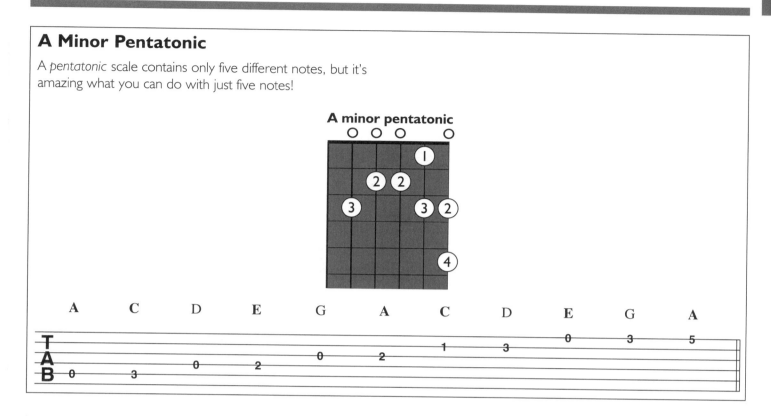

The Pull-Off

The next tune contains notes from the above A minor pentatonic scale, as well as a performance technique called the *pull-off*. This is basically the exact opposite of the hammer-on—your right hand plays the string and your left hand pulls a finger off the fretboard immediately afterwards (trying to pluck the string with the fingertip while doing so), causing the pitch to drop to either a finger on a lower fret (which needs to be already in position) or to an open string.

It's also written in a similar way to a hammer-on: a slur connects the higher note to the lower note, and a "P" is written between the staves.

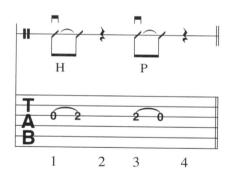

Pick a note

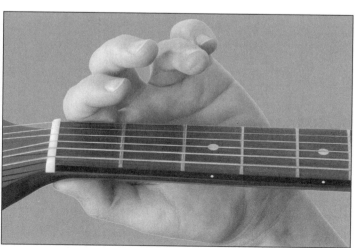

Pluck the next note with your left-hand finger

Lead Guitar

Now you're ready to get a bit funky again—use plenty of attack when you're picking the strings in this tune.

Listen to **Track 72** and then play along with **Track 73**.

Tracks 72  73

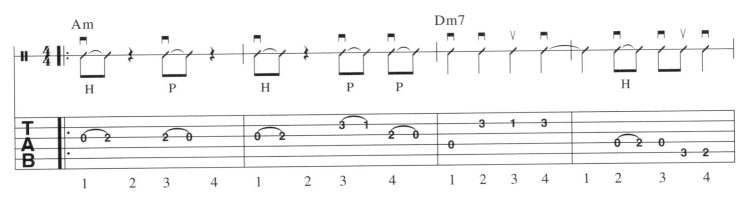

E Minor Scale

You're going to start moving your hands around the neck a little more for this next tune, and we'll throw in a few slides and grace notes in order to spice things up.

Start by practicing the following E minor scale:

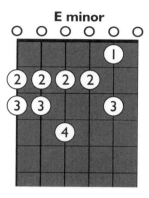

Slides

Slides are played by plucking a string and then sliding your finger up or down to the next note, written with a line from one note to the next (to show the slide) and a slur (to show that only the first of the two notes is picked).

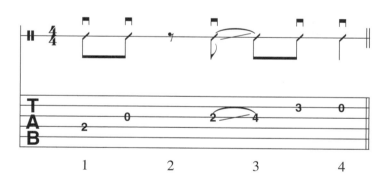

Pick a note

Slide to the next note without picking it

Grace Notes

Grace notes are the tiny notes (or numbers) written on both staves that are played very quickly (so much so that they should not really interfere with the duration of the "normal" notes). In this tune we'll use them to play very quick hammer-ons and slides.

We've included upstrokes and downstrokes on this tune, but feel free to change them if you can find a way that's more comfortable for you. Listen to this tune on **Track 74** and then try playing along with **Track 75**.

Tracks 74  75

Moveable Major Scales

It's time to move away from the bottom of the neck and look at a major scale that can be played anywhere on the fingerboard. The idea here is that you can place your first finger on any fret on the neck and play this scale in any key. Think of it as the lead guitar equivalent of a moveable bar chord!

We'll try it in *second position*, which means the first finger of your left hand should be positioned on or around the *second* fret. The first note of this scale is played on the low E string with the second finger, which in this case should be resting on the third fret, giving us a G. Here is a G major scale in second position:

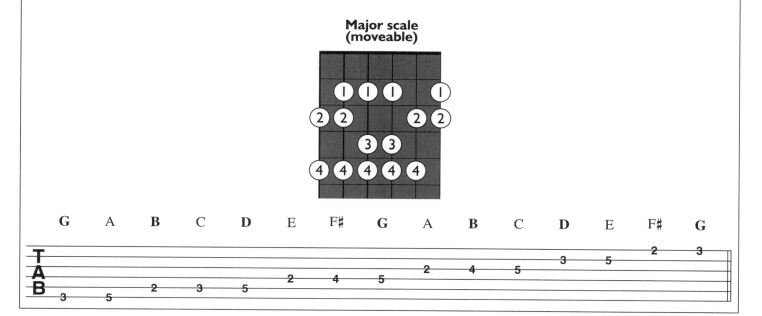

Major scale (moveable)

Before we use this scale in a tune, we'll shift it up to the seventh position (making it a C major scale) and use it in an exercise designed to make you think.

Pay close attention to what your left hand is doing here. (We've written down the correct fingerings for you.)

Try to increase your speed once you're used to it—your finger agility will improve greatly!

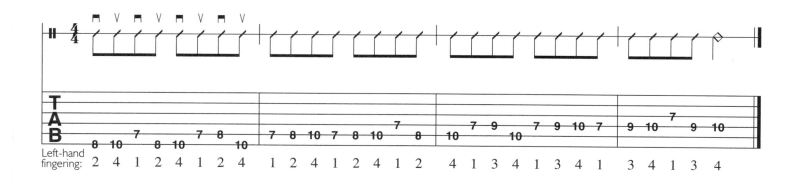

Left-hand fingering: 2 4 1 2 4 1 2 4 1 2 4 1 2 4 1 2 4 1 3 4 1 3 4 1 3 4 1 3 4

It's time to use your moveable major scale to play the wonderful old Irish folk song "The Irish Rover," with your hand in seventh position.

No fancy slides, hammer-ons, or pull-offs required here, merely clean picking and good fingering to make it sound nice. Listen to this tune on **Track 76** and then play along with **Track 77.**

THE IRISH ROVER

Tracks 76 & 77

Moveable Minor Scales

Now for a moveable minor scale, which we'll start in eighth position to give us C minor.

Be warned that you will need to shift your hand back a fret on the third string for one note (see chord box).

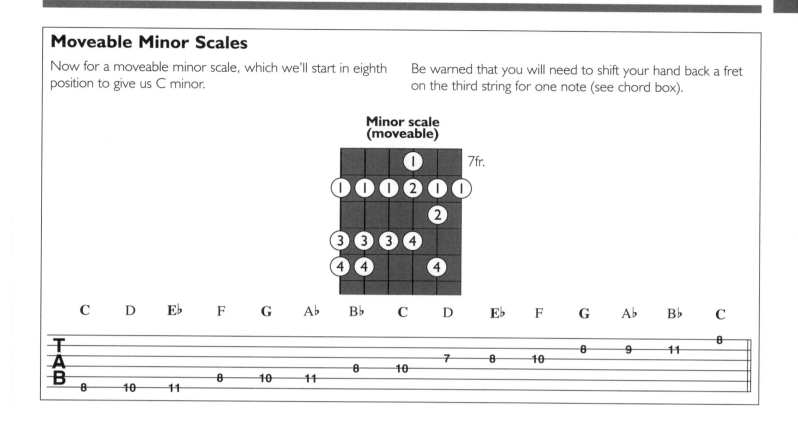

Relative Scales

A strange but useful quirk of music is the funny relationship between major and minor scales, or rather that all major scales have a *relative* minor scale (and vice versa). If you take a minor scale and start playing it from its third note up, you can hear a major scale that begins from that note. On the other hand, if you take a major scale and start playing it from its sixth note up, you can hear a minor scale beginning from that note.

This effectively means that you could use the fingering for your moveable minor scale to play any major scale you wanted. And before you start wondering, YES, you can do the same thing with the moveable major scale you just learned.

We can illustrate this more clearly on a TAB staff. Here's the same moveable minor scale used above played in the fifth position, which gives us A minor as well as C major—two scales for the price of one!

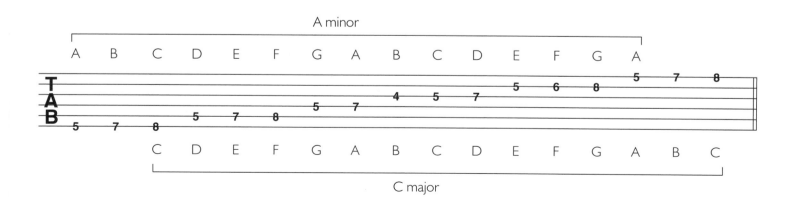

Lead Guitar

The relative major/minor principle even works with chords. We won't go into this too deeply, but as an example try playing the "standard" C major chord. Then remove your third finger (which should be on the third fret of the fifth string) and play it again.

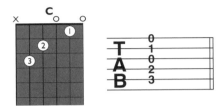

You now have Am7. It's mysteries like this that make university music professors look so stunned and bewildered all the time.

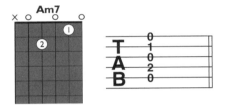

Staying in the fifth position for the moment, it's time for your playing to become a bit European. The tune on the facing page is in the French "hot club" jazz style, made famous by gypsy guitar genius Django Reinhardt and his violin-playing colleague Stéphane Grappelli around the time of World War II.

Use a swing feel for the rhythm and don't be too gentle with the pick—hot club jazz always sounds as though the guitarist is trying to snap as many strings as possible.

We're not going to make you play as fast as Django usually did—most guitar teachers can't actually play as fast as Django usually did.

Check out **Track 78** and then try it yourself with **Track 79.** Be sure to practice strumming the chords using heavy downstrokes for an authentic hot club sound.

Tracks 78  79

Swing feel

Aaah—magnifique n'est pas? (Translation: "Yeah, sounds ok I suppose…")

The Blues

You're nearly at the end, so it's time to put down your guitar, get down on your knees, bow your head and give praise to those old guitar pioneers who, many, many years ago, gave us the gift of the *blues*.

Ok, maybe you don't need to go THAT far. But blues is a truly remarkable style of music that's incredibly simple to play on guitar (whether you're playing lead or rhythm) and has provided the foundations for most guitar-based popular music since the start of the twentieth century. Get your head firmly around the blues scale and you'll find there are so many famous guitar lines (or riffs, as they're known in the trade) that you can suddenly play.

E Blues Scale in First Position

For starters, let's try an E blues scale in first position—so simple that you can do it without using your fourth finger on your left hand—simple!

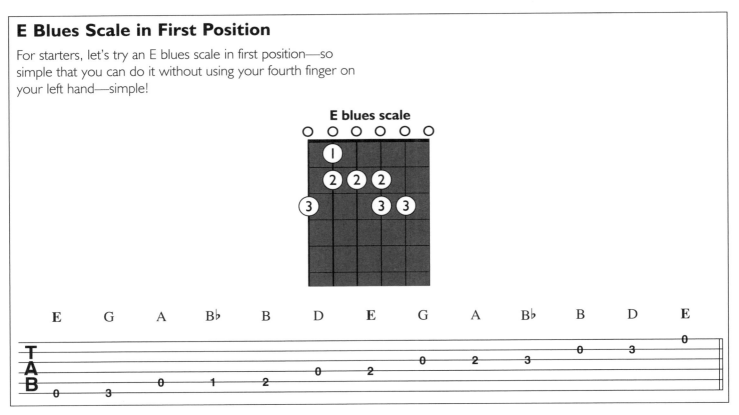

Now go back to **Track 28,** which was our basic twelve-bar blues in E (the chord progression is shown below).

Wail away over the entire tune using the E blues scale above—every note sounds good!

Track 28

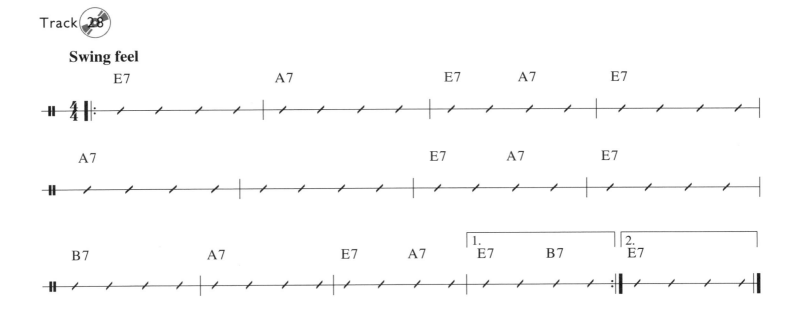

Moveable Blues Scales

Like all good scales there's also a moveable version (which uses all your fingers, but don't let that scare you). Here's an A blues scale in fifth position:

Blues scales and solos are so perfectly suited to the guitar that they practically fall out of your fingers onto the neck and strings, and you can happily spend hours fooling around with hammer-ons, pull-offs, slides, and other enhancements to your newfound "blues god" status.

Blues scale (moveable)

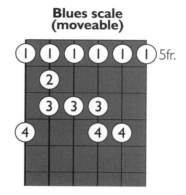

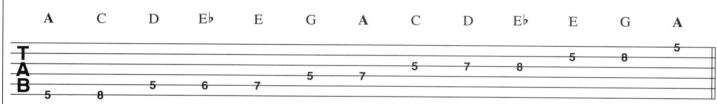

Triplets

Before you try the blues tunes in this book it's worth learning how to play a *triplet*—a useful skill to have when playing music with a swing feel (which is actually based on the triplet).

You need to fit three evenly spaced eighth notes into the duration of a quarter note (two eighth notes). So, **Example a** sounds the same as **Example b**:

Example a.

Example b.

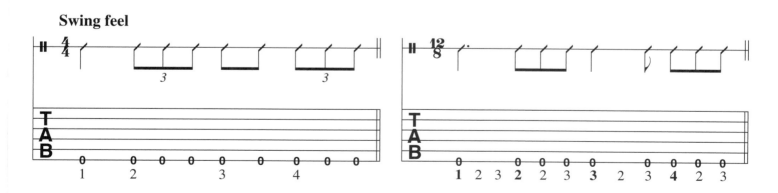

The Blues

This actually feels like a very natural thing to do when playing a swing tune, so let's try one right now.

Upstrokes and downstrokes are now up to you. Listen for the swing feel on **Track 80** and play along with **Track 81**.

BIG AL'S BLUES (VERSION 1)

Tracks 80 & 81

Swing feel

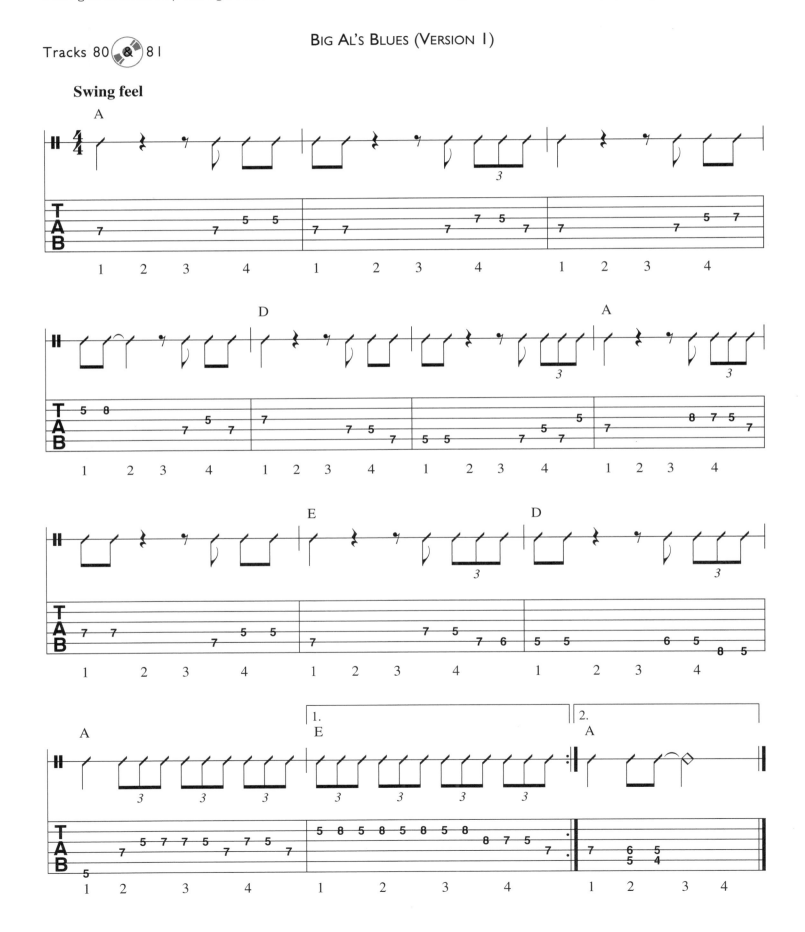

Double Stops

Most blues players will throw the occasional non–blues-scale note into their solos to add a bit more character and feel, so we're going to do the same with the next version of "Big Al's Blues" by using *double stops*, which means you will be playing two notes at a time.

The final measure (2nd time) already contains two double stops, both played with the first and second fingers. Here is where and how we'll add the others:

Measure 2

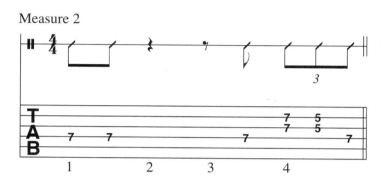

The triplet at the end of the second measure contains two double-stopped notes. Bar these with your 3rd and then 1st fingers in the same way that you fingered the original two notes. (A similar double stop occurs in measure 6.)

Measure 4

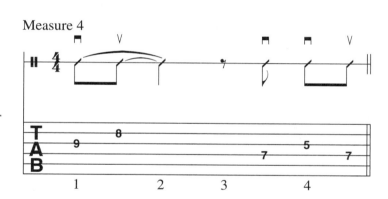

The big slur in the rhythm staff in measure 4 is a *phrase mark*—any notes within this phrase should be allowed to ring. Watch out for the slide from the 7th fret to the 9th fret on the third string.

Measure 9

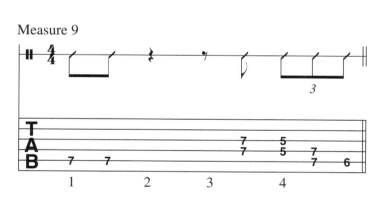

In measure 9, we have three double-stopped notes similar to those in measure 2. Bar them with your 3rd and then 1st fingers in the same way that you fingered the original three notes.

Measure 12

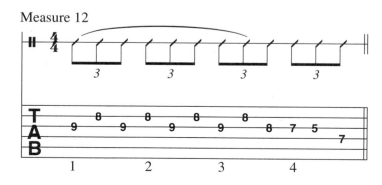

Measure 12 features another phrase mark but with multiple picking within the phrase. Slide up the 3rd string from the 7th fret to the 9th fret with the third finger as before, and allow both notes to ring.

Vibrato

A new performance effect for you is *vibrato,* where you make a note sound almost as though it's trembling as you hold it. Where you see a wobbly line (〰) drawn between the staves you should very subtly bend the string up and down extremely quickly—something that can be achieved by fretting a note, picking the string and then "wobbling" your left hand from side to side.

Wobble back…

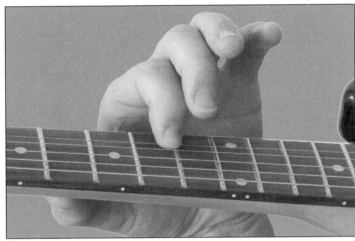

…and forth

Finally, we'll drop in a few hammer-ons, pull-offs, and grace notes to spice things up a bit! Mix all this together and you get "Big Al's Blues (Version 2)."

Listen for the tricks mentioned above on **Track 82** and then go back to **Track 81** to try it yourself.

BIG AL'S BLUES (VERSION 2)

Tracks 82 & 81

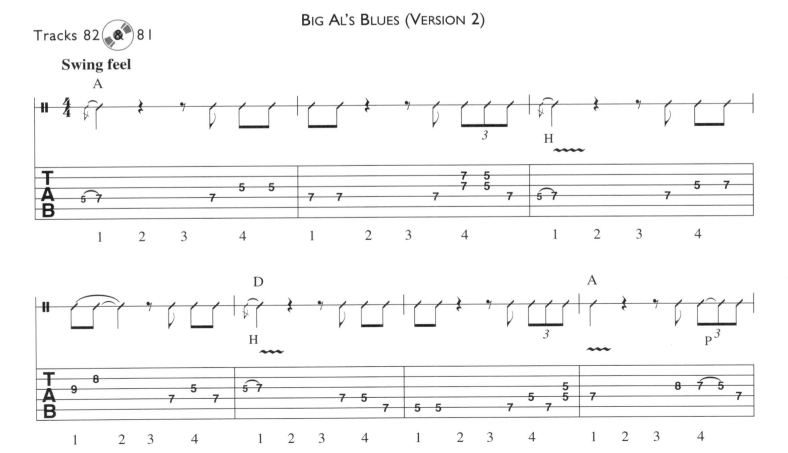

String Bending

String bends are the ultimate lead-guitar trick and an especially good effect to use with the blues. And, weird as it may sound, you can make the pitch of the string you're playing bend up OR down, contrary to all known laws of physics.

An upward string bend is achieved by having your finger ready on the fret you want to play. Pick the string with your right hand (Step 1) and push the string up toward the topside of the neck with your left hand (Step 2), causing the note to rise in pitch.

Step 1: Pick the note

Step 2: Push the string up

Downward string bends are a little trickier—the first step is to silently *pre-bend* the string (Step 2).

You then pick the string with your right hand and release the string back to its original position (Step 1).

Upward string bends are written with an arrow showing the direction of the bend from the first note to the next. The "1/2" above the arrow indicates a bend of a half step, or one fret. Push the string up until it matches the pitch of the note one fret above it. A full-step bend (two frets) would be marked "full."

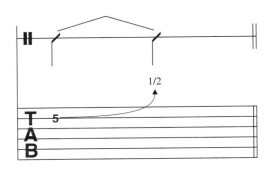

Downward string bends are written using a grace note on the TAB staff to indicate the fret that you're pre-bending up from. There is then an arrow showing the direction of the bend as you return the string to its "un-bent" state.

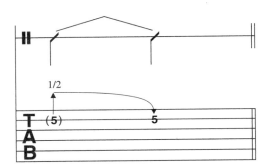

So, we've reached the end of this book. But first, here is the grande finale version of "Big Al's Blues," bursting with bends, slides, grace notes, and lots of other cool stuff to show off your newly learned guitar skills.

The string bend indication is identical in the rhythm staff for both upward and downward string bends—a big (called a *bend hat*) linking the first note to the next. Unless otherwise specified, you ONLY pick the first note of the bend.

As with slides, hammer-ons, and pull-offs, it's possible to start a string bend from a grace note, as in measure 12. Simply pick the string and bend it up very quickly, then release the bend as normal.

Measure 12

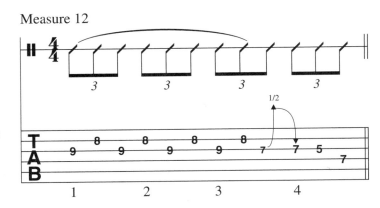

I hope that you have enjoyed learning from this book—it's been fun. However, it is now time for you to fly the nest, get out there into the big wide world, and share your guitar god/goddess status with anyone who will listen. Good luck!

BIG AL'S BLUES (FINALE)

Tracks 83 & 81

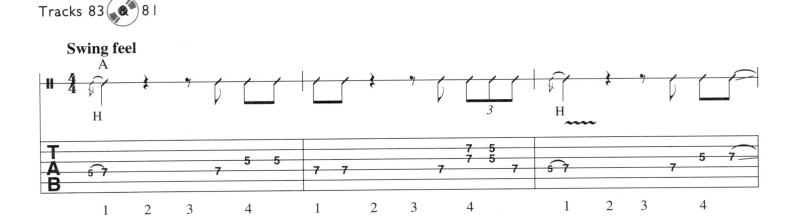

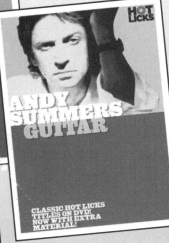